the herb kitchen

the herb kitchen

A COLLECTION OF FRESH AND FRAGRANT RECIPES

Consultant Editor: Emma Summer

LORENZ BOOKS

First published in 1999 by Lorenz Books

Lorenz Books is an imprint of
Anness Publishing Limited
Hermes House
88-89 Blackfriars Road
London SE1 8HA

This edition distributed in Canada by
Raincoast Books
8680 Cambie Street
Vancouver
British Columbia V6P 6M9

ISBN 0 7548 0260 4

A CIP catalogue record for this book is available from the British Library

Publisher Joanna Lorenz
Senior Cookery Editor Linda Fraser
Project Editor Emma Gray
Jacket Designer Luise Roberts
Designers Lilian Lindblom and Bill Mason
Illustrations Anna Koska

Recipes Catherine Atkinson, Alex Barker, Angela Boggiano, Carla Capalbo, Kit Chan, Jacqueline Clark, Maxine Clark, Frances Cleary, Andi Clevely, Carole Clements, Roz Denny, Nicola Diggins, Joanna Farrow, Rafi Fernandez, Christine France, Silvano Franco, Sarah Gates, Shirley Gill, Carole Handslip, Deh-Ta Hsiung, Shezad Husain, Christine Ingram, Patricia Lousada, Ruby Le Bois, Sue Maggs, Norma Miller, Janice Murfitt, Annie Nichols, Maggie Pannell, Katherine Richmond, Liz Trigg, Hilaire Walden, Stuart Walton, Laura Washburn, Steven Wheeler, Kate Whiteman, Elizabeth Wolf-Cohen and Jeni Wright
Photographers Karl Adamson, William Adams-Lingwood, Edward Allwright, David Armstrong, Steve Baxter, James Duncan, John Freeman, Michelle Garrett, Amanda Heywood, David Jordan, Don Last, Thomas Odulate, Patrick McLeavey, Michael Michaels
Food for photography Jacqueline Clark, Joanna Farrow, Carole Handslip, Jane Hartshorn, Katherine Hawins, Wendy Lee, Lucy McKelvie, Jane Stevenson
Stylists Madeleine Brehaut, Diana Civil, Hilary Guy, Clare Hunt, Maria Kelly, Blake Minton, Marian Price, Kirsty Rawlings, Jenny Shapter, Fiona Tillett, Judy Williams, Elizabeth Wolf-Cohen

For all recipes, quantities are given in both metric and imperial measures and, where appropriate, measures are also given in standard cups and spoons. Follow one set, but not a mixture, because they are not interchangeable. Use medium eggs unless otherwise stated.

Printed and bound in Singapore

1 3 5 7 9 10 8 6 4 2

contents

INTRODUCTION

One of the most rewarding ways of flavouring food – and giving a familiar dish a unique signature – is by the judicious use of herbs. There's something very satisfying about stepping outside on a warm summer evening to snip fresh chives, coriander, chervil and young sorrel leaves to add to a green salad, sprigs of tarragon to put on your roasting chicken, or big bunches of parsley for an authentic tabbouleh. Reach for a couple of bay leaves to garnish a terrine or flavour a winter stew and you are instantly transported back to the sunny morning when you picked them and hung them to dry in your kitchen.

Most herbs are easy to grow, demanding little more than a sunny position and light, well-drained soil. Whether you have a garden plot or just a few herbs on the windowsill, being able to pick your own herbs and use them instantly, when the essential oils are at their most flavoursome, is richly rewarding. This has now been recognized by the majority of retailers, many of whom will sell several different varieties of the most used herbs already growing in pots.

Dried herbs are more pungent than their fresh counterparts. You only need between one-third to half the quantity. This can be a drawback; dried herbs you seldom use may have lost much of their flavour by the time the jar is empty, so store them carefully, away from direct sunlight, and check the jars often. Buy little and often and throw away any herbs that have become tasteless or musty, or that you know are more than a few months old.

The best way to familiarize yourself with culinary herbs is to be adventurous and to experiment with all sorts of different herbs; ask friends and family what their favourite combinations are, or vary the herbs in a familiar recipe. Although some herbs have a natural affinity with certain foods (rosemary with lamb, sage with pork, dill with fish or basil with tomatoes), it is quite often the unexpected combination that produces the most exciting results. Chicken with Red Pesto, for instance, or Coriander Crab with Coconut are just two of the many tempting recipes that feature in this book. From soups, savouries and salads to sweets and refreshing drinks, this book issues an invitation to explore the wonderful world of culinary herbs.

Kitchen Herbs

Using fresh instead of dried herbs for a dish can create quite a different taste. Fresh herbs have a lighter flavour and a wonderful aromatic quality that is unrivalled by any dried herb.

Basil

Known for its affinity with tomatoes, basil is also excellent with fish, pasta and egg dishes.

Cultivation: Sow the seeds indoors in spring. Plant out in a sunny position in well-drained soil after any danger of frost and snow is passed.

Bay

The dried leaves are used in stews, soups, casseroles and many milk puddings.

Cultivation: Needs fertile and well-drained soil in quite a sheltered and sunny position. Can be grown in a pot. Prune to shape in summer.

Chives

Use chives as a garnish for soups and salads, with cottage cheese or in omelettes.

Cultivation: Grows in almost any type of soil. Propagate by dividing it in spring or autumn and replanting clumps of about six little bulbs.

Coriander

The aromatic leaves add a hint of spice to salads, vegetables and some Eastern desserts.

Cultivation: Sow seeds in spring in warm, dry soil in a sunny position. Be quite careful not to overwater the plants, especially when young.

DILL

The leaves are used with fish and the seeds for cabbage dishes, marinades and pickles. Its name comes from the Norse word *dilla*, which means "to lull", indicating one of its properties.

Cultivation: Sow seeds in spring. They will need thinning out as dill requires a lot of space to grow. Water the seeds when the soil is dry to the touch.

LEMON BALM

This lemon-flavoured herb, which looks very similar to mint, is quite delicious in creamy white sauces for fish, poultry or pork. It is also a good flavouring for summer drinks, including water.

Cultivation: A hardy, herbaceous perennial, it grows in any soil, self-seeding freely. Cuttings left in water will root readily. Lemon Balm thrives in full sun.

LOVAGE

A large glossy-leaved hardy perennial, lovage has clusters of yellow flowers in summer and reaches a height of 2.1m/7ft. Add leaves to soups and stews; the stems can be candied like angelica.

Cultivation: Planted in a rich, well-drained soil, lovage can become a striking feature in any herb garden, and will will need very little care and attention.

MARJORAM

A cultivated variety of oregano, with a milder but distinctive flavour. Use with lamb, poultry, in stuffings, egg, milk and cheese dishes. It combines well with peppers, chilli, garlic, onions and tomatoes.

Cultivation: Sow seeds under cover in autumn. Plant them in spring in rich soil in full sun with midday shade. Cut the plants back by two-thirds in the autumn.

OREGANO

Although known as the "pizza herb", oregano is not used solely for this purpose. It is widely used in Italian and Mexican cooking, and goes well with meats, tomatoes, courgettes, eggs and cheese.

Cultivation: Some species of oregano are half-hardy and others will tolerate frost. Choose a suitable variety. They need a well-drained soil, and are quite easy to propagate by division.

PARSLEY

Curly or flat leafed, parsley has a wonderful clean taste. Try it in salads, soups, stuffings and deep fried as a special garnish. A herb that is rich in vitamins A and C, iron and antioxidants.

Cultivation: Plant in moist soil in a partially shaded site. Cut the leaves as needed to promote new growth. In the second year it is quick to flower and needs cutting early.

PEPPERMINT

The leaves are very dark green, sometimes purple, with intensely aromatic leaves. The oil can be used to flavour confectionery, liqueurs and syrups. Peppermint makes an excellent tea if infused in boiling water.

Cultivation: Mint prefers cool damp situations, but will grow and spread almost anywhere. Those with very small gardens should keep mint in pots as it has a vigorous habit .

ROSEMARY

The spiky leaves of this pungent herb look like tiny pine needles. Use sparingly in soups, stews or vegetable dishes or insert, with slivers of garlic, under the skin of lamb or chicken before roasting.

Cultivation: Propagate from seeds sown in spring, or from semi-ripe cuttings in summer. Plant them in a sunny position in a sheltered spot. Prune back some time in the autumn.

Sage

These soft, velvety grey-green leaves, set in pairs are particularly good with pork, in stuffings (commonly used with onion) and with liver. Its name comes from the Latin *salvere,* which means "to cure".

Cultivation: Sage grows best in light, dry soil. Purple sage is mostly hardy, but the tricolour sage should be given winter protection. Sage is propagated from cuttings or by layering.

Spearmint

Do not reserve this refreshing herb for mint sauce. Try it sprinkled over leafy green salads, tomato soup or even grapefruit. Spearmint is often used in savoury and sweet dishes. The smell is menthol.

Cultivation: Grow spearmint in containers if you are a little concerned about it spreading or if the soil is too dry. It is very easy to propagate any type of mint from runners and cuttings.

Tarragon

Tarragon has a faintly aniseed taste that is used to flavour vinegars, oils, fish dishes, sauces (such as Béarnaise, for example), chicken and salad dressings. It is delicious chopped and sprinkled on salads.

Cultivation: Propagate by dividing roots in mid-spring. Cuttings can also be taken from the spring growth. Keep young plants under glass until the frosts are definitely over.

Thyme

The tiny leaves are widely used in stuffings and many different savoury recipes. Thyme goes well with meat, tomato, egg and cheese dishes. It is an essential ingredient in bouquets garnis.

Cultivation: Thyme likes to be planted in well-drained, limy soil in an open sunny position. In late summer, clip thyme back to encourage a cushion-like, compact and bushy habit.

USING HERBS

PICKING

Harvest herbs often – early in the morning is best. Remove the outer leaves of parsley and chervil first and pick out the tops of basil frequently to stop the plant flowering too early.

DRYING

Herbs are best dried naturally, hung in an airy passageway or kitchen, or laid on a wire rack. They can also be dried overnight in an oven heated to the lowest temperature, then turned off. Strip off the dried leaves from the stems and store whole or crumbled in airtight jars.

CHOPPING

Use either a sharp broad-bladed knife or a mezzaluna (a curved blade with a handle at either end) for chopping herbs. The simplest way to chop small amounts of parsley and similar herbs is to put them in a mug and snip them using a pair of sharp scissors.

FREEZING

Chopped or finely snipped tarragon, mint, chives and basil freeze well. Pack them in ice-cube trays, fill with water and freeze until solid, then wrap in clear film, label and return to the freezer for up to 6 months.

HERB BUTTER

For a savoury butter: put the butter in a mixing bowl and beat with a wooden spoon or electric mixer until soft. Add the flavouring. Season savoury butter to taste with salt and pepper. Blend well.

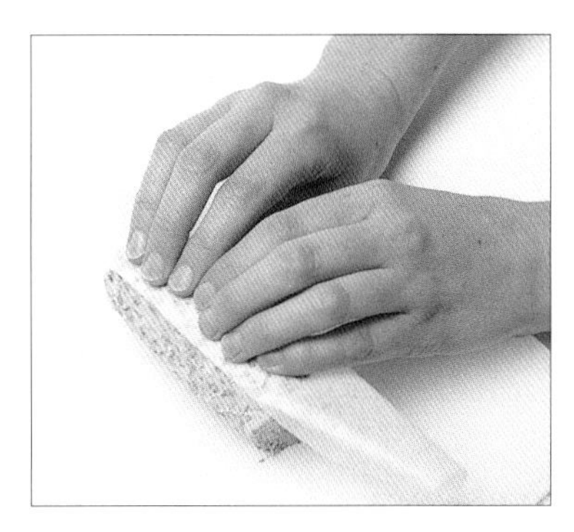

Transfer the butter to a piece of waxed paper and shape it into a neat roll, handling it as little as possible, to keep the butter cool. Wrap and refrigerate until firm. Cut into discs.

BOUQUET GARNI

Make your own bouquet garni by tying together a bay leaf and a sprig each of thyme, marjoram and parsley.

TIME-SAVING TIP

To dry fresh herbs in the microwave, spread the clean sprigs in an even layer between several sheets of kitchen paper and microwave on High (100% power) for 2 minutes. Rearrange the herbs, cover with fresh kitchen paper and cook for about 2 minutes more, checking the herbs every 30 seconds and removing them from the microwave as soon as they appear dry. Leave to cool and dry completely. Never leave the microwave unattended when drying herbs.

HERBAL OILS

Capture the very essence of herbs in oils which you can then use as ingredients in your cooking. Use a fine virgin olive oil. This can be used in salad dressings and in other dishes as well as for frying. Decant the flavoured oils into attractively shaped or coloured bottles.

MAKING HERB OILS

Herbs should be collected in the morning after the dew has dried, but before the flavours have dissipated in the hot sun. Allow the moisture from the freshly-picked herbs to evaporate completely before use, otherwise they may become mouldy. Pour the oil into a wide-topped jar and add a large handful of herbs. Allow to steep for two weeks, then strain and decant into a pretty bottle. Remember to label each bottle with the herbs used to make it.

MIXED HERB OIL

Steep sage, rosemary, tarragon and marjoram in virgin olive oil, then decant the oil into a clean bottle. Bind a selection of the herbs with string and tie around the neck of the new bottle. Use to pan-fry chicken or to make herby salad dressings.

DILL AND LEMON OIL

Steep a handful of fresh dill and a large strip of lemon rind in virgin olive oil, then decant. Label, or tie a slice of dried lemon around the neck of the bottle to indicate the flavour. Use to pan-fry or grill fish. This oil can also be used for salad dressings.

THYME OIL

Steep a handful of thyme in virgin olive oil, then decant. Tie two large sprigs of thyme to the bottle for decoration. Excellent for brushing over chicken before roasting or as a glaze for herb scones.

MEDITERRANEAN HERB OIL

Steep rosemary, thyme and marjoram in virgin olive oil, then decant. Decorate the bottle with herbs tied around a cinnamon stick. Add to garlicky tomato sauces, and to *coq au vin* or lamb *daubes*. This oil can be used in most Mediterranean dishes.

BASIL AND CHILLI OIL

Steep basil and three chillies in virgin olive oil, then decant into a clean bottle. You could draw basil and chilli on a label to indicate the contents of the bottle. Add to tomato and mozzarella salads. This oil is delicious brushed over Italian-style breads.

Right: Bottles of herb oils. For storage the herbs are removed from the oil which is then decanted into new bottles.

JAMES
MARS

HERBAL VINEGARS

Herb-flavoured vinegars give a delicious depth and variety to salad dressings and many savoury dishes and, if they are used sparingly, will enhance the flavour of fruit such as strawberries and nectarines that are not quite ripe. Use the vinegars within three months of making.

MAKING HERB VINEGARS

Heat the vinegar in a saucepan for a few minutes. If using spices, add them now and leave for about five minutes to allow the flavours to infuse, then pour the hot liquid over the herbs. Cover the mixture with a square of muslin, and leave for a few days in a cool, dark place, such as a cupboard, larder or outhouse, stirring occasionally. Using the muslin, strain off the vinegar from the herbs and spices and pour it into a clean dry bottle, add a sprig or two of the herbs used to flavour the vinegar to denote the flavour and finally seal the bottle with a cork.

Herb vinegars are very easy to make and it is worth experimenting with your own favourite flavours. The ratio of herb to vinegar can be varied to produce milder or stronger flavours, with surprisingly successful results.

RASPBERRY AND LEMON THYME VINEGAR

Add 15ml/1 tbsp of pickling spice to 600ml/1 pint/2½ cups of red wine vinegar, heat for 5 minutes. Pour the vinegar on to 450g/1 lb raspberries and two sprigs of fresh lemon thyme. This makes a delicious, sweet and aromatic herb vinaigrette dressing. A little neat vinegar is also very good used with many bland fruits to accentuate their flavour.

LEMON, LIME AND MARJORAM VINEGAR

Bring 600ml/1 pint/2½ cups of white wine vinegar to the boil then pour it over the rind of one unwaxed, lemon, one unwaxed lime and a small bunch of marjoram. Cover and leave to infuse for three days. Strain and pour into a clean, dry bottle, adding fresh rind for colour. Citrus vinegars are wonderful for piquant sauces, such as hollandaise.

ROSEMARY VINEGAR

Bring 600ml/1 pint/2½ cups cider vinegar to the boil in a saucepan, then pour it over 90ml/6 tbsp of fresh, chopped rosemary. Cover, and leave to infuse for three days. Strain, and pour it into a clean, dry bottle, adding a sprig of rosemary for decoration. Herb vinegars are excellent for adding flavour to dressings and sauces.

Right: Bottles of herb vinegars with the herbs infusing. Try using different types of vinegars to vary the basic flavour.

starters, dips and salsas

Herbs bring a vibrant freshness and colour to soups and combine brilliantly with a variety of fish, shellfish, poultry and vegetables to make a range of dishes suitable for serving at the beginning of a main meal, as part of a buffet or, in the case of salsas, as accompaniments.

Chick-pea and Parsley Soup

This tasty soup, served with a tangy lemon garnish, comes from Morocco, where parsley is a favourite ingredient. If possible, use flat leaf parsley.

Serves 6

225g/8oz/1¼ cups chick-peas, soaked overnight
1 small onion
40g/1½oz fresh flat leaf parsley
30ml/2 tbsp olive and sunflower oil, mixed
1.2 litres/2 pints/5 cups chicken stock
juice of ½ lemon
salt and freshly ground black pepper
lemon wedges and finely pared strips of rind, to garnish
crusty bread, to serve

Cook's tip

Chick-peas blend better in soups and other dishes if you rub away the outer skin. Although this will take you some time, it is worth the effort as the soup will be smoother.

Drain the chick-peas and rinse under cold water. Cook them in plenty of boiling water for 1–1½ hours until tender. Drain and peel (see Cook's Tip).

Place the onion and parsley in a blender or food processor and blend until finely chopped. Alternatively, chop each very finely and mix together. Heat the olive and sunflower oils in a saucepan or flameproof casserole and fry the onion mixture for 3–4 minutes over a low heat until the onion is slightly softened. Add the chick-peas, cook gently for 1–2 minutes and add the stock. Season well with salt and pepper. Bring the soup to the boil, then cover and simmer for 20 minutes until the chick-peas are very tender.

Allow the soup to cool a little and then part-purée in a blender or food processor, or mash with a fork, so that the soup is thick but still chunky.

Return the soup to a clean pan, add the lemon juice and adjust the seasoning if necessary. Heat gently and then serve garnished with lemon wedges and finely pared rind, and accompanied by crusty bread.

CEP SOUP WITH PARSLEY CROUTONS

The little parsley croûtons add a mild, herby flavour to this delicious and unusual soup.

Serves 4

50g/2oz/4 tbsp butter

2 onions, finely chopped

1 garlic clove

225g/8oz fresh ceps or button mushrooms, trimmed and sliced

75ml/5 tbsp dry white wine

900ml/1½ pints/3¾ cups boiling chicken stock

115g/4oz floury potatoes, peeled and diced

1 thyme sprig

15ml/1 tbsp lemon juice

salt and freshly ground black pepper

For the parsley croûtons

50g/2oz/4 tbsp butter

3 slices day-old bread, cut into 2.5cm/1in fingers

45ml/3 tbsp finely chopped fresh parsley

Melt the butter in a large saucepan and fry the onions for 4–5 minutes until lightly browned. Add the garlic, mushrooms and wine, stir briefly then add the stock, potatoes and thyme. Simmer gently for 45 minutes.

Pour the soup into a blender or food processor and blend briefly so that pieces of mushroom are left intact. Transfer the soup to a clean pan, add the lemon juice and season to taste.

Make the croûtons. Melt the butter in a large frying pan and add the fingers of bread. Fry for 2–3 minutes until golden and then stir in the parsley. Ladle the soup into warmed soup bowls, add the parsley croûtons and serve.

Italian Bean and Parsley Soup

Italian flat leaf parsley adds a fresh, aromatic flavour to this well-flavoured and hearty soup.

Serves 6

175g/6oz/1 cup dried haricot beans, soaked overnight

1.75 litres/3 pints/7½ cups chicken stock or water

115g/4oz/1 cup pasta shells

60ml/4 tbsp olive oil, plus extra, to serve

2 garlic cloves, crushed

60ml/4 tbsp chopped fresh flat leaf parsley

salt and freshly ground black pepper

Cook's tip

Use medium-size pasta shells or shapes for this recipe. If using fresh pasta, simmer for just 5–6 minutes until the pasta is tender.

Drain the beans and place in a large saucepan with the stock or water. Bring to the boil, boil rapidly for 10 minutes, then lower the heat and simmer, half-covered for 2–2½ hours until the beans are tender. Spoon half of the beans and a little of their cooking liquid into a blender or food processor and blend until smooth. Stir back into the remaining beans in the pan.

Add the pasta and simmer gently for 15 minutes until the pasta is tender, adding a little extra water or stock if the soup seems too thick.

Heat the oil in a small pan and fry the garlic until golden. Stir into the soup with the parsley and season well with salt and pepper. Ladle into warmed soup bowls and drizzle each with a little extra olive oil.

Cauliflower and Coriander Soup

Light and tasty, this spicy coriander-flavoured soup makes a wonderfully warming first course, an appetizing quick meal or – when served chilled – a delicious summertime treat.

Serves 4–6

15ml/1 tbsp sunflower oil
1 large potato, peeled and diced
1 small cauliflower, chopped
1 onion, chopped
1 garlic clove, crushed
15ml/1 tbsp grated fresh root ginger
10ml/2 tsp ground turmeric
5ml/1 tsp cumin seeds
5ml/1 tsp black mustard seeds
10ml/2 tsp ground coriander
1 litre/1¾ pints/4 cups vegetable stock
300ml/½ pint/1¼ cups natural yogurt
salt and ground black pepper
fresh coriander or parsley, to garnish

Heat the oil in a large saucepan, add the potato, cauliflower and onion and toss to coat. Drizzle over 45ml/3 tbsp water. Heat until hot and bubbling, then cover and turn the heat down. Continue cooking the mixture for about 10 minutes.

Stir in the garlic, ginger, seeds and spices. Cook for 2 minutes more, stirring occasionally. Pour in the stock and add plenty of salt and pepper. Bring to the boil, then lower the heat, cover and simmer for about 20 minutes. Stir in the yogurt, adjust the seasoning and garnish with coriander or parsley. Serve at once.

CARROT AND CORIANDER SOUP

For maximum flavour, young carrots are best. Coriander accentuates their sweetness in this recipe.

Serves 5–6

15ml/1 tbsp sunflower oil
1 onion, chopped
675g/1½lb carrots, chopped
2–3 fresh coriander sprigs or 5ml/1 tsp dried coriander
5ml/1 tsp grated lemon rind
30ml/2 tbsp lemon juice
900ml/1½ pints/3¾ cups chicken stock
salt and ground black pepper
chopped fresh coriander, to garnish

COOK'S TIP

This soup freezes well. After blending the mixture, cool it quickly, then pour it into a carton or similar container for freezing. Remember to allow a little headroom as the soup will expand on freezing.

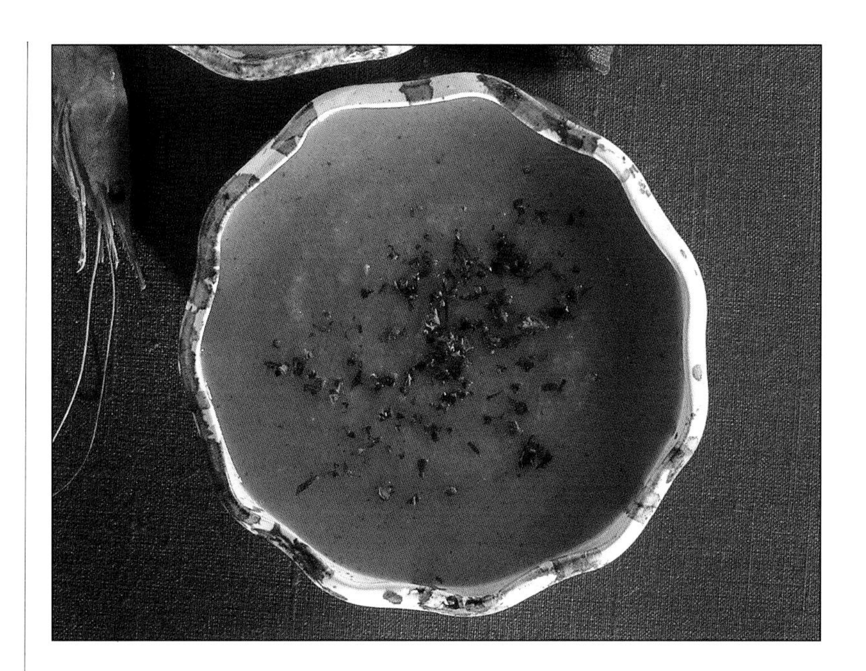

Heat the oil in a large saucepan. Fry the onion over a gentle heat for 5 minutes, until softened but not coloured. Add the chopped carrots, coriander sprigs or dried coriander, lemon rind and juice. Stir well, then add the chicken stock with salt and pepper to taste.

Bring to the boil, lower the heat, cover and simmer for 15–20 minutes, occasionally checking that there is sufficient liquid. When the carrots are really tender, purée the mixture in a blender or food processor. Return to the pan, then check the seasoning.

Heat through again. Sprinkle with chopped coriander before serving.

VEGETABLE SOUP WITH PISTOU

One of France's best-known specialities, Vegetable Soup with Pistou owes its flavour to Provençal produce and homemade basil pesto.

Serves 4–6

1 courgette, diced
1 small potato, diced
1 shallot, chopped
1 carrot, diced
225g/8oz can chopped tomatoes
1.2 litres/2 pints/5 cups vegetable stock
50g/2oz French beans, cut into 1cm/½in lengths
50g/2oz/½ cup frozen petits pois
50g/2oz/½ cup small pasta shapes
60–90ml/4–6 tbsp homemade or bought pesto
15ml/1 tbsp sun-dried tomato paste
salt and ground black pepper
freshly grated Parmesan cheese, to serve

Place the courgette, potato, shallot, carrot and tomatoes in a large saucepan. Add the vegetable stock and season with salt and pepper. Bring to the boil, then lower the heat, cover and simmer for 20 minutes.

Add the French beans, petits pois and pasta. Cook for 10 minutes more, until the pasta is tender. Adjust the seasoning.

Ladle the soup into warmed individual bowls. Mix together the pesto and sun-dried tomato paste, and stir a spoonful into each serving. Serve with grated Parmesan cheese to sprinkle into each bowl.

MINTED YOGURT AND CUCUMBER SOUP

Mint brings an extra lift to this creamy Middle Eastern-style cold soup – perfect for a summer lunch.

Serves 4

1 large cucumber, peeled
300ml/½ pint/1¼ cups single cream
150ml/¼ pint/⅔ cup natural yogurt
2 garlic cloves, crushed
30ml/2 tbsp white wine vinegar
15ml/1 tbsp chopped fresh mint
salt and ground black pepper
sprigs of fresh mint, to garnish

Grate the cucumber coarsely. Place in a bowl with the cream, yogurt, garlic, vinegar and mint. Stir well and season to taste.

Chill for at least 2 hours. Just before serving, stir the soup again. Pour into individual bowls and garnish with mint sprigs.

TOMATO AND BASIL TARTS

These crisp little tartlets are easy to make and, as ever, basil and tomato make a winning combination.

Serves 4

2 sheets of filo pastry

1 egg white

75g/3oz/scant ½ cup cream cheese

1 handful of fresh basil leaves

3 small tomatoes, sliced

salt and ground black pepper

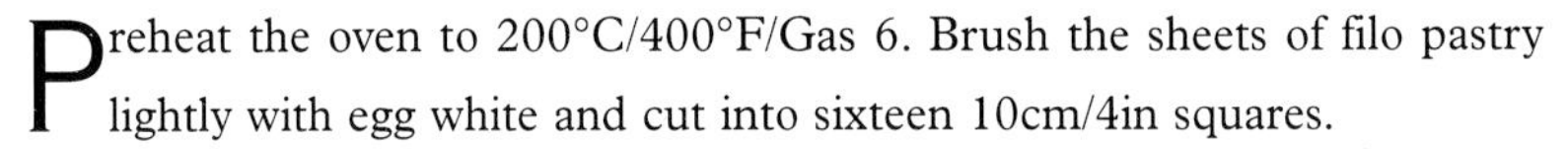

Preheat the oven to 200°C/400°F/Gas 6. Brush the sheets of filo pastry lightly with egg white and cut into sixteen 10cm/4in squares.

Place the squares in eight muffin tins, using a double layer each time. Beat the cheese until it is creamy, then divide it among the filo cases. Season with black pepper and top with basil leaves.

Arrange the tomato slices on the tarts, add salt and pepper to taste, and bake for 10–12 minutes, until golden. Serve warm, fresh from the oven.

COOK'S TIP

Egg white has been used for the filo pastry in order to cut down on the amount of fat in the tarts. Use melted butter or oil, if you prefer.

CHERRY TOMATOES WITH GUACAMOLE AND CORIANDER

Cherry tomatoes stuffed with a creamy coriander-flavoured guacamole make perfect nibbles.

Makes 24

24 cherry tomatoes

1 large ripe avocado

50g/2oz/¼ cup cream cheese

3–4 dashes of Tabasco sauce, or to taste

grated rind and juice of ½ lime

30ml/2 tbsp chopped fresh coriander

salt

COOK'S TIP

The tomatoes can be prepared the day before. Store in the fridge, ready for filling, upside down in a covered tub. Don't be tempted to make the guacamole ahead of time, though, as it may discolour.

Cut a slice from the bottom of each tomato, then use the handle of a small spoon to scoop out the seeds. Sprinkle the cavities with salt. Drain the tomatoes upside down on kitchen paper for at least 30 minutes.

Cut the avocado in half and discard the stone. Scoop the flesh into a food processor or blender and add the cream cheese. Process until very smooth, scraping down the sides of the bowl once or twice. Season with salt and Tabasco sauce, then add the lime rind and juice. Toss in half of the chopped coriander and process to blend.

Spoon the mixture into a piping bag fitted with a medium star nozzle. Pipe swirls into the tomatoes. Arrange on a platter, sprinkle with the remaining coriander and serve.

Smoked Salmon Pancakes with Basil Pesto

Mini pesto-flavoured pancakes are topped with crème fraîche, smoked salmon and fresh basil to create this delicious bite-size starter.

Makes 12–16

120ml/4fl oz/½ cup milk
125g/4oz/1 cup self-raising flour
1 egg
30ml/2 tbsp homemade or bought pesto
vegetable oil, for frying
200ml/7fl oz/scant 1 cup crème fraîche
75g/3oz smoked salmon
15g/½oz/1 tbsp pine nuts, toasted
12–16 fresh basil sprigs, to garnish

Pour half of the milk into a mixing bowl. Add the flour, egg and pesto. Mix to a smooth batter, then add the rest of the milk and stir until it is evenly blended.

Heat the vegetable oil in a large frying pan. Spoon the pancake mixture into the heated oil in small heaps. Allow about 30 seconds for the pancakes to rise, then turn and cook briefly on the other side. Continue cooking the pancakes in batches until all the batter is used up.

Arrange the pancakes on a serving plate and top each one with a spoonful of crème fraîche. Cut the salmon into 1cm/½in strips and place on top of each pancake. Add a scattering of pine nuts and garnish each pancake with a fresh basil sprig.

Cook's Tip

The pancakes are ready for turning when tiny bubbles appear on the surface.

GRILLED PARSLEY MUSSELS

This is a really great tapas dish. The parsley and Parmesan make a fantastic topping and you'll find they are devoured the moment they are ready!

Serves 4

450g/1lb fresh mussels
15ml/1 tbsp melted butter
15ml/1 tbsp olive oil
45ml/3 tbsp freshly grated Parmesan cheese
30ml/2 tbsp chopped fresh parsley
2 garlic cloves, finely chopped
2.5ml/½ tsp coarsely ground black pepper

Scrub the mussels thoroughly, pulling away the gritty beards. Discard any mussels that don't close when sharply tapped with a knife.

Place the mussels and 45ml/3 tbsp water in a large pan. Cover and steam for 5–6 minutes until all the mussels have opened. Drain, discarding any that remain closed.

Remove and discard the top shell of each mussel. Place the mussels in a flameproof dish, packing them closely together so that they stay level. Preheat the grill to high.

Mix together the melted butter, olive oil, Parmesan, parsley, garlic and black pepper. Spoon a little of this mixture on top of each mussel and grill for 2–3 minutes until the mussels are sizzling and golden. Serve the mussels in their shells.

COOK'S TIP

This is a dish to serve to good friends as it can be rather messy! Remember to give guests napkins to wipe the juices off their chins.

FRIED CLAMS WITH BASIL AND CHILLIES

This delectable combination of clams, basil and chillies comes from Thailand, where it can often be found on the menu at seaside restaurants.

Serves 4

1kg/2¼lb fresh clams
30ml/2 tbsp vegetable oil
4 garlic cloves, finely chopped
15ml/1 tbsp grated fresh root ginger
4 shallots, finely chopped
30ml/2 tbsp yellow bean sauce
6 red chillies, seeded and chopped
15ml/1 tbsp fish sauce
pinch of granulated sugar
1 handful of basil leaves, plus extra to garnish

Wash and scrub the clams. Heat the oil in a wok or large frying pan. Add the garlic and ginger and fry for 30 seconds, then add the shallots and fry for 1–2 minutes more.

Add the clams. Using a fish slice or spatula, turn them a few times to coat with the oil. Stir in the yellow bean sauce and half the red chillies.

Continue to cook, stirring often, for 5–7 minutes, or until all the clams open. You may need to add a splash of water. Adjust the seasoning with fish sauce and a little sugar.

Finally, add the basil and transfer to individual warmed bowls or a platter. Garnish with the remaining red chillies and basil leaves.

COOK'S TIP

Fresh clams are usually available all year round, but you may need to order them from the fishmonger.

HOT CORIANDER PRAWNS

Don't stint on the coriander when making this hot and spicy starter. Added at the last minute, it retains its flavour and colour better.

Serves 4–6

1 garlic clove, crushed
1cm/½in piece of fresh root ginger, peeled and chopped
1 small fresh red chilli, seeded and chopped
10ml/2 tsp sugar
15ml/1 tbsp light soy sauce
15ml/1 tbsp vegetable oil
5ml/1 tsp sesame oil
juice of 1 lime
salt, to taste
675g/1½lb whole raw prawns
175g/6oz/1 cup cherry tomatoes
½ cucumber, cut into chunks
1 small bunch of coriander, roughly chopped

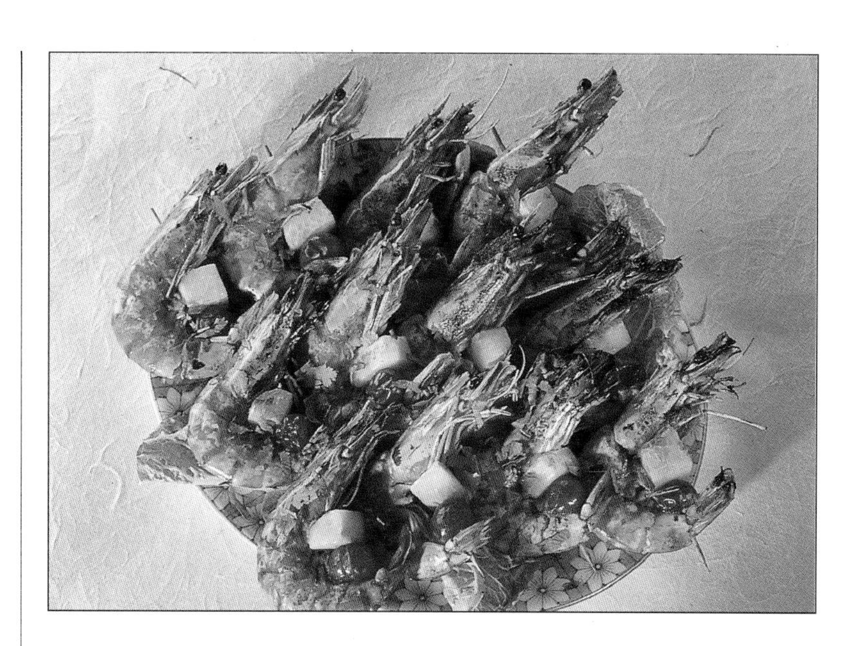

Combine the garlic, ginger, chilli and sugar in a mortar and pound to a paste with a pestle. Add the soy sauce, vegetable and sesame oils, lime juice and salt. Arrange the prawns in a single layer in a shallow dish, pour over the marinade and coat well. Cover and marinate for as long as possible, preferably 8 hours.

Preheat the grill. Drain the prawns and thread them on to bamboo skewers, alternately with the tomatoes and cucumber. Grill for 3–4 minutes, brushing occasionally with any remaining marinade. Transfer to a platter, scatter with the coriander and serve.

PRAWN "POPCORN" WITH BASIL MAYONNAISE

One of the most compelling reasons for visiting Louisiana is to taste the wonderful Cajun cooking. This dish of spiced prawns and basil mayonnaise comes from there and it is truly irresistible.

Serves 8

900g/2lb raw prawns, peeled and deveined
2 eggs, beaten
250ml/8fl oz/1 cup dry white wine
50g/2oz/½ cup fine cornmeal
50g/2oz/½ cup plain flour
15ml/1 tbsp finely snipped fresh chives
1 garlic clove, crushed
2.5ml/½ tsp fresh thyme leaves
1.5ml/¼ tsp salt
1.5ml/¼ tsp cayenne pepper
1.5ml/¼ tsp ground black pepper
oil, for deep-frying

For the mayonnaise

1 egg yolk
10ml/2 tsp Dijon mustard
15ml/1 tbsp white wine vinegar
250ml/8fl oz/1 cup olive oil
25g/1oz/½ cup fresh basil leaves, finely shredded
salt and ground black pepper

Rinse the prawns in a sieve under cold running water. Drain well and set aside in a cool place. Mix the eggs and wine in a small bowl.

In a mixing bowl, combine the cornmeal and flour, chives, garlic, thyme, salt, cayenne and pepper. Gradually whisk in the egg mixture to make a smooth batter. Cover and leave to stand for 1 hour at room temperature.

Make the mayonnaise. Combine the egg yolk, mustard and vinegar in a mixing bowl. Add salt and pepper to taste. Add the oil in a thin stream, beating vigorously with a wire whisk. When the mixture is thick and smooth, stir in the basil. Cover and chill until ready to serve.

Heat oil to a depth of 5–7.5cm/2–3in in a large frying pan or deep-fryer to about 185°C/360°F, or until a small piece of dry bread sizzles as soon as it is added to the pan. Dip the prawns into the batter and fry in small batches for 2–3 minutes, or until golden brown. Turn as necessary for even colouring. Remove with a slotted spoon and drain on kitchen paper. Serve hot, with the basil mayonnaise.

CHICKEN STICKS WITH CORIANDER DIP

A refreshing coriander yogurt makes the perfect dipping sauce for these Tandoori-style chicken sticks.

Makes about 25

175ml/6fl oz/¾ cup natural yogurt
5ml/1 tsp garam masala or curry powder
1.5ml/¼ tsp ground cumin
1.5ml/¼ tsp ground coriander
1.5ml/¼ tsp cayenne pepper
5ml/1 tsp tomato purée
1–2 garlic cloves, finely chopped
2.5cm/1in piece of fresh root ginger, peeled and finely chopped
grated rind and juice of ½ lemon
30ml/2 tbsp chopped fresh coriander or mint
450g/1lb boneless, skinless chicken breasts

For the coriander dip

250ml/8fl oz/1 cup natural yogurt
30ml/2 tbsp whipping cream
½ cucumber, peeled, seeded and finely chopped
30ml/2 tbsp chopped fresh coriander or mint
salt and ground black pepper

Prepare the coriander dip first. Combine all the ingredients in a bowl and season with salt and ground black pepper. Cover and chill until ready to serve.

Put the yogurt, spices, tomato purée, garlic, ginger, lemon rind and juice and herbs in a food processor or blender, and process until smooth. Pour into a shallow dish.

Freeze the chicken breasts for 5 minutes to firm them slightly, then slice them in half horizontally. Cut the slices into 2cm/¾in strips and add to the marinade. Toss to coat well. Cover and chill for 6–8 hours or overnight.

Preheat the grill and line a baking sheet with foil. Using a slotted spoon, remove the chicken from the marinade and arrange the pieces in a single layer on the baking sheet. Scrunch up the chicken slightly so it makes wavy shapes. Grill for 4–5 minutes until brown and just cooked, turning once. Thread 1–2 pieces on to cocktail sticks or short skewers and serve with the coriander dip.

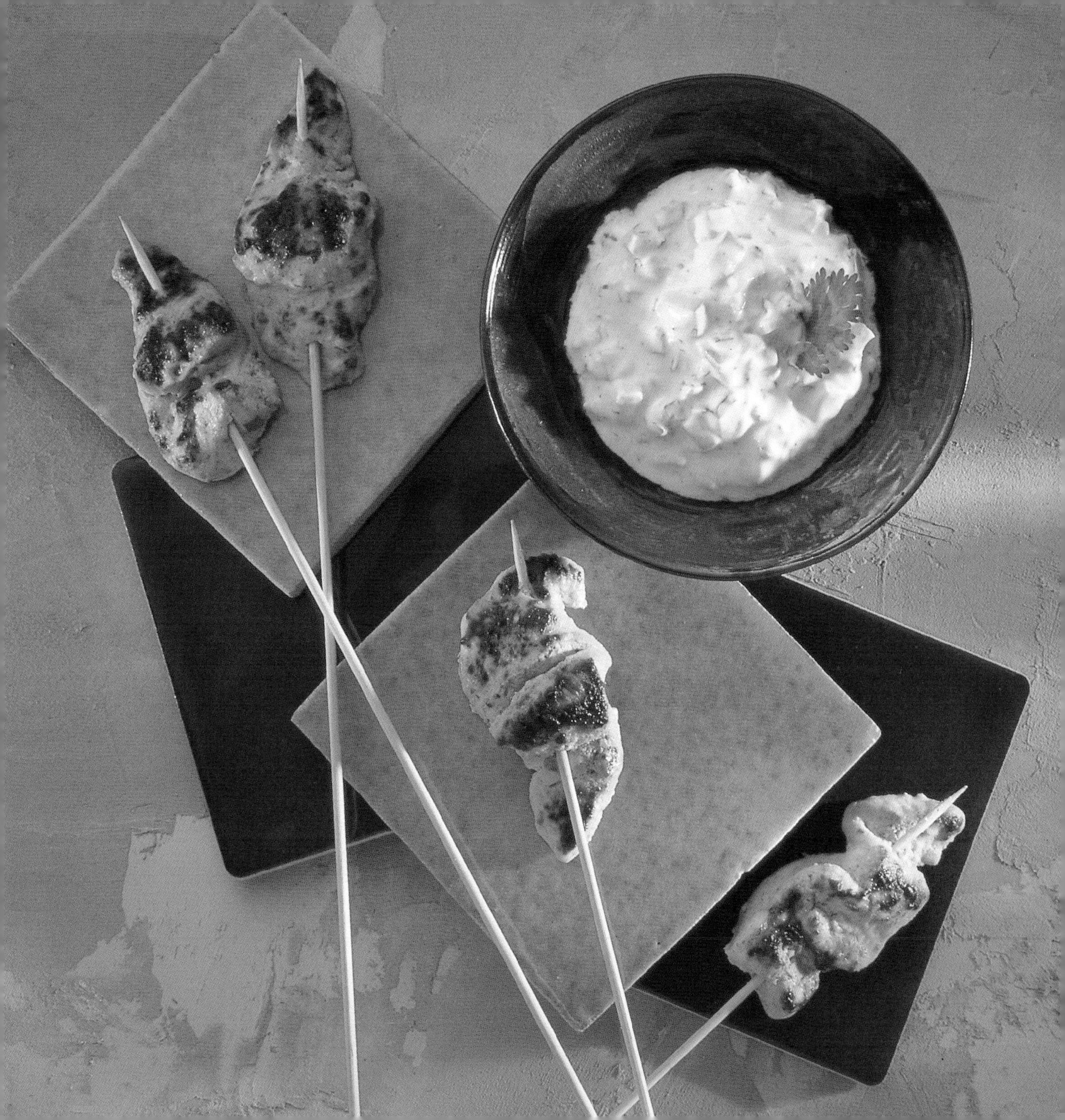

CRUNCHY MUSHROOMS WITH DILL DIP

These crisp bites are ideal as an informal starter or served with drinks.

Serves 4–6

115g/4oz/2 cups fresh fine white breadcrumbs
25ml/1½ tbsp finely grated mature Cheddar cheese
5ml/1 tsp paprika
225g/8oz button mushrooms
2 egg whites

For the tomato and dill dip

4 ripe tomatoes
115g/4oz/½ cup curd cheese
60ml/4 tbsp natural low-fat yogurt
1 garlic clove, crushed
30ml/2 tbsp chopped fresh dill
salt and ground black pepper
dill sprig, to garnish

Preheat the oven to 190°C/375°F/Gas 5. Mix the breadcrumbs, cheese and paprika together in a bowl.

Wipe the mushrooms clean and trim the stalks, if necessary. Lightly whisk the egg whites with a fork, until frothy.

Dip each mushroom into the egg whites, then into the breadcrumb mixture. Repeat until all the mushrooms are coated.

Place the mushrooms on a non-stick baking sheet. Bake in the preheated oven for 15 minutes, or until tender and the coating has turned golden and crunchy.

To make the dip, score the bases of the tomatoes with a sharp knife. Plunge them into a saucepan of boiling water for 1 minute, then into a saucepan of cold water. Remove the skins. Halve the tomatoes, remove the seeds and cores and roughly chop the flesh.

Put the curd cheese, yogurt, garlic clove and dill into a mixing bowl and stir to combine thoroughly. Season to taste with salt and black pepper. Add the chopped tomatoes and stir to combine. Spoon the mixture into a serving dish and garnish with a sprig of fresh dill. Serve the mushrooms hot, together with the dip.

COOL MINT RAITA

This refreshing minty dish is the ideal antidote to any spicy food, especially fiery Indian curries.

Serves 4

7 large sprigs of fresh mint
1 small onion
½ cucumber
300ml/½ pint/1¼ cups natural yogurt
2.5ml/½ tsp salt
2.5ml/½ tsp sugar
pinch of chilli powder

Tear the leaves from the stalks of 6 of the mint sprigs and chop finely. Peel and very thinly slice the onion, separating it into rings. Cut the cucumber into 5mm/¼in dice.

Mix together the chopped mint, onion, cucumber, yogurt, salt and sugar. Spoon into a serving bowl and chill.

Just before serving sprinkle with chilli powder and garnish with the remaining mint sprig.

COOK'S TIP

This also makes a deliciously fresh dip for crudités. Use Greek-style yogurt for a creamier texture and add some crushed garlic for extra flavour. Serve with raw fresh vegetables cut into matchstick strips or tortilla chips.

Salsa Verde

This is a classic salsa, made with chillies, onions and plenty of fresh parsley.

Serves 4

2–4 green chillies, seeded
8 spring onions, trimmed and halved
2 garlic cloves, halved
50g/2oz salted capers
fresh tarragon sprig
40g/1½oz fresh parsley
grated rind and juice of 1 lime
90ml/6 tbsp olive oil
about 15ml/1 tbsp green Tabasco sauce, to taste
freshly ground black pepper

Cook's tip

If you can only find capers pickled in vinegar, rinse well in cold water before using.

Place the chillies, spring onions and garlic in a blender or food processor and blend briefly until the ingredients are roughly chopped. Rub the excess salt off the capers, but do not rinse them. Add the capers to the chilli and onion mixture, together with the tarragon and parsley. Blend again until finely chopped.

Transfer the mixture to a small bowl and stir in the lime rind and juice and olive oil. Stir briefly to mix. Add the green Tabasco sauce and black pepper. Chill in the fridge until ready to serve, but do not prepare more than 8 hours in advance.

TOMATO AND BACON SALSA

This distinctive tomato salsa is sharpened with lime juice and fresh coriander. The smoky bacon adds an extra dimension to the flavour and, with soured cream, it makes a delicious filling for baked potatoes.

Serves 4

450g/1lb tomatoes
15ml/1 tbsp sunflower oil
4 smoked streaky bacon rashers, finely chopped
45ml/3 tbsp chopped fresh coriander leaves
1 garlic clove, finely chopped
juice of 1 lime
salt and freshly ground black pepper
baked potatoes topped with butter or soured cream, to serve

COOK'S TIP

For an extra kick, add a dash of hot pepper sauce or a pinch of dried chillies to the salsa.

Peel the tomatoes by plunging them into boiling water for 30 seconds. Refresh in cold water and then peel away the skins. Cut into quarters and remove the cores and seeds. Finely chop the flesh and place in a bowl.

Heat the oil in a frying pan and fry the bacon pieces for 5 minutes until crisp and golden, stirring occasionally. Allow to cool and then mix with the tomatoes. Add the coriander, garlic and lime juice and season with salt and pepper. Transfer to a serving bowl and chill. Serve with baked potatoes topped with butter or soured cream.

Chunky Cherry Tomato Salsa

Succulent cherry tomatoes and refreshing cucumber form the base of this delicious, dill-seasoned salsa.

Serves 4

1 cucumber
5ml/1 tsp sea salt
500g/1¼lb cherry tomatoes
juice and grated rind of 1 lemon
45ml/3 tbsp chilli oil
2.5ml/½ tsp dried chilli flakes
1 garlic clove, finely chopped
30ml/2 tbsp chopped fresh dill
salt and freshly ground black pepper

Trim the ends from the cucumber, cut into 2.5cm/1in lengths and then cut each piece lengthways into thin slices. Place in a colander and sprinkle with sea salt. Set aside for 5 minutes until the cucumber has wilted. Wash the cucumber well under cold water and pat dry with kitchen paper.

Quarter the cherry tomatoes and place in a bowl with the cucumber. Place the lemon rind and juice, chilli oil, chilli flakes, garlic and dill in a small jug. Season with salt and pepper and whisk with a fork. Pour the chilli oil dressing over the tomato and cucumber and toss well. Leave to marinate at room temperature for at least 2 hours before serving.

COOK'S TIP

Try flavouring this salsa with other fragrant herbs, such as fresh tarragon, coriander or even mint.

vegetable and vegetarian dishes

Bring out the best in succulent fresh vegetables by partnering them with the right herbs. From classics such as Beans with Parsley Sauce to the exotic Vegetables in Coconut Milk and Basil, to substantial vegetarian dishes like Vegetable Cannelloni with Rosemary or Nut and Coriander Pilaff, there is something here for every taste.

STUFFED PARSLEY ONIONS

The tasty parsley stuffing goes perfectly with roasted onions. Serve as part of a vegetarian meal or as an accompaniment to roast meat or chicken.

Serves 4

4 large onions
60ml/4 tbsp cooked rice
20ml/4 tsp finely chopped fresh parsley, plus extra to garnish
60ml/4 tbsp grated Chedddar cheese
30ml/2 tbsp olive oil
about 15ml/1 tbsp white wine, to moisten
salt and freshly ground black pepper

COOK'S TIP

The onion centres can be used in soups or for other dishes. However, uncooked cut onion does not keep well, so use on the same day or discard.

Preheat the oven to 180°C/350°F/Gas 4. Cut a slice from the top of each onion and scoop out the centre, leaving a fairly thick shell. Blend together the cooked rice, parsley, cheese, olive oil and seasoning, moistening with enough wine to mix well.

Fill the onions and bake in the oven for 45 minutes. Serve garnished with a sprinkling of chopped parsley.

LEEKS WITH PARSLEY DRESSING

The parsley dressing gives these leeks a wonderful flavour. Serve French-style as a salade tiède *(warm salad), with grilled or poached fish and new potatoes.*

Serves 4

700g/1½lb young leeks

For the dressing

25g/1oz fresh flat leaf parsley

30ml/2 tbsp olive oil

juice of ½ lemon

50g/2oz/½ cup broken walnuts, toasted

5ml/1 tsp caster sugar

1 hard-boiled egg, shelled

salt and freshly ground black pepper

Cut the leeks into 10cm/4in lengths and rinse well to remove any grit or soil. Bring a saucepan of salted water to the boil and simmer the leeks for 8 minutes. Drain and rinse in cold water to cool slightly and then drain again thoroughly.

Make the dressing. Reserve a sprig or two of parsley for the garnish and put the remainder in a blender or food processor. Blend until finely chopped, add the olive oil, lemon juice and toasted walnuts and blend again for 1–2 minutes until smooth. Add about 90ml/6 tbsp water to make a smooth sauce and add sugar and seasoning to taste.

Arrange the leeks on a serving plate and spoon over the sauce. Finely grate the hard-boiled egg and scatter over the sauce. Serve at room temperature, garnished with the reserved parsley.

ROSEMARY ROASTIES

These unusual roast potatoes, cooked in their skins, are given an extra lift by the addition of rosemary.

Serves 4

900g/2lb small red potatoes
10ml/2 tsp walnut or sunflower oil
30ml/2 tbsp fresh rosemary leaves
salt and paprika
fresh rosemary sprigs, to garnish

Preheat the oven to 240°C/475°F/Gas 9.

Leave the potatoes whole with the peel on; if large, cut in half. Place the potatoes in a large pan of cold water and bring to the boil. Drain them well.

Drizzle the walnut or sunflower oil over the potatoes and shake the pan to coat them evenly.

Tip the potatoes into a shallow roasting tin. Sprinkle with rosemary, salt and paprika. Roast for 30 minutes or until crisp. Garnish and serve hot.

ROSEMARY ROSTI

Rosemary is an excellent partner for potatoes in this tasty, traditional Swiss dish.

Serves 4

350g/12oz par-cooked potatoes
45ml/3 tbsp olive oil
10ml/2 tsp chopped fresh rosemary
pinch of freshly grated nutmeg
75g/3oz smoked bacon, cut into cubes
salt flakes and ground black pepper
fresh rosemary sprigs, to garnish
4 quails' eggs, to serve

Coarsely grate the potatoes and thoroughly pat dry on kitchen paper to remove all the moisture.

Heat a heavy-based frying pan, then add 30ml/2 tbsp of the oil. When the oil is hot, add the potatoes and cook them in batches until crisp and golden. This will take about 10 minutes. Drain them on kitchen paper, mix with the rosemary, nutmeg and plenty of seasoning and keep warm.

Add the bacon to the hot frying pan and stir-fry until crisp. Sprinkle the bacon on top of the potato.

Heat the frying pan again and add the remaining oil. When the oil is hot, fry the quails' eggs for about 2 minutes. Make a pile of the rosemary rosti, garnish with sprigs of fresh rosemary and serve with the eggs.

COOK'S TIP

Serve this dish for a hearty and warming winter breakfast or as an unusual starter to a family meal – hungry, growing children love it.

BAKED MARROW IN PARSLEY SAUCE

This creamy parsley sauce is a really glorious way of enriching a simple and modest vegetable.

Serves 4

1 small young marrow, about 900g/2lb

30ml/2 tbsp olive oil

15g/½oz/1 tbsp butter

1 onion, chopped

15ml/1 tbsp plain flour

300ml/½ pint/1¼ cups milk and single cream, mixed

30ml/2 tbsp chopped fresh parsley

salt and freshly ground black pepper

Preheat the oven to 180°C/350°F/Gas 4 and cut the marrow into rectangular pieces, about 5 x 2.5cm/2 x 1in. Heat the oil and butter in a flameproof casserole and fry the onion over a gentle heat until very soft. Add the marrow and sauté for 1–2 minutes, then stir in the flour. Cook for a few minutes and stir in the milk and cream mixture.

Add the parsley and seasoning and stir well to mix. Cover and cook in the oven for 30–35 minutes. Serve hot.

COOK'S TIP

If liked, remove the lid for the final 5 minutes of cooking to gratinize the top of the dish.

Baked Courgettes with Mint

Creamy yet tangy goat's cheese combines with fresh mint to make simple baked courgettes into a special dish.

Serves 4

8 small courgettes, weighing about 450g/1lb in total
15ml/1 tbsp olive oil, plus extra for greasing
75–115g/3–4oz goat's cheese, cut into thin strips
1 small bunch fresh mint, finely chopped
ground black pepper

Preheat the oven to 180°C/350°F/Gas 4. Cut out eight rectangles of foil large enough to encase each courgette and brush each with a little oil.

Trim the courgettes and cut a thin slit along the length of each. Insert pieces of goat's cheese in the slits. Add a little mint and sprinkle with the olive oil and black pepper.

Wrap each courgette in a foil rectangle, place on a baking sheet and bake for about 25 minutes until tender.

Cook's Tip

The many different types of goat's cheese vary from smooth and fresh-tasting to very strong and tangy, but if you don't like the flavour, you could substitute a milder cheese, such as mozzarella, Pecorino or mild Cheddar.

Vegetable and Basil Kebabs

Vegetables nestling in basil and mint leaves make great kebabs – choose any vegetables in season.

Serves 4

24 mushrooms
16 cherry tomatoes
16 thick slices of courgette
16 squares of red pepper
16 basil leaves, plus extra to garnish
16 large mint leaves

To baste

115g/4oz/½ cup butter, melted
1 garlic clove, crushed
15ml/1 tbsp crushed green peppercorns
salt

For the sauce

50g/2oz/¼ cup butter
45ml/3 tbsp brandy
250ml/8fl oz/1 cup double cream
5ml/1 tsp crushed green peppercorns

Thread the vegetables on to eight skewers, placing the basil leaves next to the tomatoes, and wrapping the mint leaves around the courgette slices. Preheat the grill or prepare the barbecue.

Mix the basting ingredients and baste the kebabs thoroughly. Place the skewers under the grill or on a grid over medium-hot coals, turning and basting regularly for about 5–7 minutes until the vegetables are just cooked.

Heat the butter for the sauce in a frying pan, then add the brandy and light it. When the flames have died down, stir in the cream and the peppercorns. Cook for about 2 minutes, stirring all the time. Serve the kebabs with the green peppercorn sauce, garnished with basil.

Spiced Aubergine with Mint Yogurt

A minty yogurt sauce is the perfect complement to aubergines cooked with mixed spices.

Serves 4

2–3 aubergines
30–45ml/2–3 tbsp olive oil
5ml/1 tsp ground cumin
5ml/1 tsp ground coriander
1.25ml/¼ tsp chilli powder
150ml/¼ pint/⅔ cup Greek-style yogurt
1 garlic clove, crushed
30ml/2 tbsp chopped fresh mint, plus extra to garnish
salt and ground black pepper

Cook's Tip

Dégorging or salting the aubergine slices helps to extract the bitter juices.

Slice the aubergines thickly and place in a shallow dish. Sprinkle with salt and leave to drain for 30 minutes. Rinse the aubergine slices and pat dry thoroughly with kitchen paper.

Arrange the aubergines on a baking sheet and brush with oil. Sprinkle over half of each spice. Cook under a hot grill until softened and browned.

Turn over the aubergine slices, brush again with oil and sprinkle with the remaining spices. Grill for a further 4–5 minutes, until the second sides are browned.

Meanwhile, make the mint yogurt. Mix together the yogurt, crushed garlic and mint and season to taste with plenty of freshly ground black pepper. Spoon into a small serving bowl.

Arrange the grilled aubergines on a serving plate, sprinkle with chopped mint and serve with the mint yogurt.

VEGETABLES IN COCONUT MILK AND BASIL

This delectable way of cooking vegetables comes from Thailand. Adding the basil at the last minute produces a mouth-watering aroma.

Serves 4–6

450g/1lb mixed vegetables, such as aubergines, baby sweetcorn, carrots, fine green beans, patty pan squash
8 fresh red chillies, seeded and roughly chopped
2 lemon grass stalks, chopped
4 kaffir lime leaves, torn
30ml/2 tbsp vegetable oil
250ml/8fl oz/1 cup coconut milk
30ml/2 tbsp fish sauce
salt
15–20 Thai basil leaves, to garnish

Cut the mixed vegetables into even shapes of similar size. Put the red chillies, lemon grass and kaffir lime leaves in a mortar and grind to a paste with a pestle.

Heat the oil in a wok. Add the chilli paste and fry for 2–3 minutes, then stir in the coconut milk and bring to the boil. Add the vegetables and cook for about 5 minutes, or until they are tender. Season with the fish sauce and salt and garnish with basil leaves.

COOK'S TIP

If you don't like highly spiced food, use fewer red chillies.

PARSLEYED VEGETABLE RIBBONS

Brie and parsley combine to make a delicately flavoured sauce to serve with these elegant vegetables.

Serves 4

15ml/1 tbsp sunflower oil
1 large green pepper, cored and diced
225g/8oz Brie cheese
30ml/2 tbsp crème fraîche
5ml/1 tsp lemon juice
60ml/4 tbsp milk
10ml/2 tsp freshly ground black pepper
2–3 fresh parsley sprigs
6 large courgettes
6 large carrots
chopped fresh parsley, to garnish

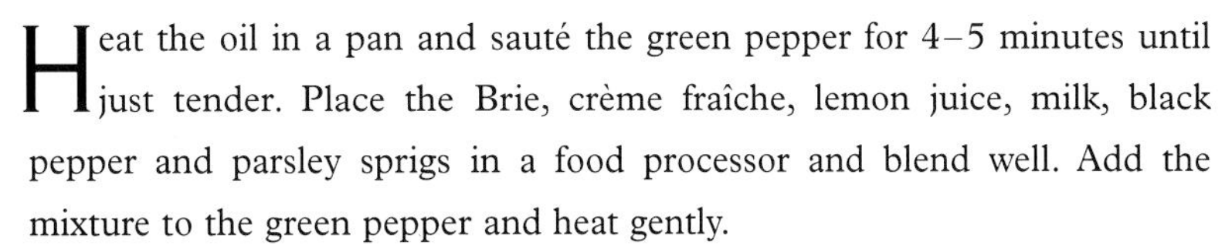

Heat the oil in a pan and sauté the green pepper for 4–5 minutes until just tender. Place the Brie, crème fraîche, lemon juice, milk, black pepper and parsley sprigs in a food processor and blend well. Add the mixture to the green pepper and heat gently.

Using a potato peeler, slice the courgettes and carrots into thin strips. Place them in separate saucepans with enough water to cover and simmer for 3 minutes until just tender. The courgettes will take 2–3 minutes, the carrots a little longer. Drain.

Pour the warm sauce into a shallow serving dish. Add the courgettes and carrots and toss carefully to coat in the sauce. Garnish with a little finely chopped parsley and serve.

FRESH MINTED VEGETABLE STEW

A spiced dish of mixed vegetables, with the addition of fresh mint, this aromatic stew can be served as a side dish or as a vegetarian main course.

Serves 4–6

45ml/3 tbsp vegetable stock
1 green pepper, seeded and sliced
2 medium courgettes, sliced
2 medium carrots, sliced
2 celery sticks, sliced
2 medium potatoes, diced
400g/14oz can chopped tomatoes
5ml/1 tsp chilli powder
30ml/2 tbsp chopped fresh mint
15ml/1 tbsp ground cumin
400g/14oz can chick-peas, drained
salt and ground black pepper
fresh mint leaves, to garnish

COOK'S TIP

Chick-peas are traditional in this type of Middle Eastern dish, but if you prefer, red kidney beans or haricot beans can be used instead.

Heat the vegetable stock in a large flameproof casserole until boiling, then add the sliced pepper, courgettes, carrots and celery. Stir over a high heat for 2–3 minutes, until the vegetables are beginning to soften.

Add the potatoes, tomatoes, chilli powder, mint and cumin. Add the chick-peas and bring to the boil.

Reduce the heat, cover the casserole and simmer for 30 minutes, or until all the vegetables are tender. Season to taste with salt and pepper and serve hot, garnished with mint leaves.

BEANS WITH PARSLEY SAUCE

In this classic dish the parsley sauce is enriched with egg yolks and double cream.

Serves 4

20g/¾oz/1½ tbsp butter

900g–1.2kg/2–2½lb fresh broad beans, shelled

1 large parsley sprig

150ml/¼ pint/⅔ cup double or whipping cream

3 egg yolks

a few drops of lemon juice

30ml/2 tbsp chopped fresh parsley

salt and freshly ground black pepper

Melt the butter in a saucepan and stir in the beans. Cook for 2–3 minutes, then add the parsley sprig, seasoning and enough water just to cover the beans. Cover the pan tightly, bring to boiling point and then immediately lower the heat and cook very gently for 15–20 minutes, shaking the pan occasionally, until the beans are tender and no liquid remains. Remove the pan from the heat, discard the parsley and leave to cool slightly.

Mix the cream with the egg yolks and stir into the beans. Reheat gently, stirring all the time, until the sauce coats the back of the spoon: do not boil.

Add a few drops of lemon juice and adjust the seasoning. Sprinkle with the chopped parsley and serve.

COOK'S TIP

If the beans are not as fresh as you would like and if you have the time and patience, slip off the outer skin of each bean. The bright green inner bean is wonderfully sweet and tender.

VEGETABLES WITH CIDER AND MINT

The cider sauce is also ideal for other vegetables, such as celery or beans. It is flavoured with tamari, a Japanese soy sauce, and applemint.

Serves 4

1 large onion, chopped
2 large carrots, chopped
1 large garlic clove
15ml/1 tbsp dill seeds
4 large sprigs of applemint
30ml/2 tbsp olive oil
30ml/2 tbsp plain flour
300ml/½ pint/1¼ cups dry cider
450g/1lb broccoli florets
450g/1lb cauliflower florets
30ml/2 tbsp tamari
10ml/2 tsp mint jelly

Sauté the onion, carrots, garlic, dill seeds and applemint in the olive oil until the vegetables are nearly cooked. Stir in the flour and cook for about 30 seconds. Pour in the cider and simmer until the sauce looks glossy.

Boil the broccoli and cauliflower in separate pans until tender.

Pour the sauce into a food processor and add the tamari and the mint jelly. Blend until finely puréed. Drain the broccoli and cauliflower and transfer to a serving dish. Pour over the sauce and serve.

Beansprouts with Coriander

This simple, delicious dish is given extra zest by the addition of fresh coriander. For the freshest results, sprout your own beans.

Serves 3–4

30ml/2 tbsp sunflower or groundnut oil
225g/8oz beansprouts
2 spring onions, chopped
1 garlic clove, crushed
30ml/2 tbsp soy sauce
10ml/2 tsp sesame oil
15ml/1 tbsp sesame seeds
30ml/2 tbsp chopped fresh coriander
salt and ground black pepper

Cook's Tip

You can buy beans for sprouting from most health food shops. Follow the directions on the packet to produce your own sprouts for this stir-fry. Beansprouts can be stored in the fridge for up to two days.

Heat the oil in a large wok and stir-fry the beansprouts, spring onions and garlic for 3–5 minutes.

Add the soy sauce, sesame oil, sesame seeds and chopped coriander, with plenty of salt and pepper to taste. Toss over the heat for 1–2 minutes more and serve.

Coriander and Vegetable Stew

Coriander is used in combination with chick-peas and aubergine in this spicy West African stew.

Serves 3–4

45ml/3 tbsp olive oil
1 red onion, chopped
3 garlic cloves, crushed
115g/4oz sweet potatoes, peeled and diced
1 large aubergine, diced
425g/15oz can chick-peas, drained
5ml/1 tsp dried tarragon
2.5ml/½ tsp dried thyme
5ml/1 tsp ground cumin
5ml/1 tsp ground turmeric
2.5ml/½ tsp ground allspice
5 drained canned plum tomatoes, chopped, plus 60ml/4 tbsp of the can juices
6 ready-to-eat dried apricots
600ml/1 pint/2½ cups vegetable stock
1 fresh green chilli, seeded and finely chopped
30ml/2 tbsp chopped fresh coriander
salt and ground black pepper

Heat the olive oil in a large saucepan over a medium heat. Add the onion, garlic and sweet potatoes and cook for about 5 minutes until the onion has softened slightly.

Stir in the diced aubergine, then add the chick-peas and the herbs and spices. Stir well to mix and cook over a gentle heat for a few minutes.

Add the tomatoes and the reserved juice from the can, with the apricots, stock and chilli. Stir in salt and pepper to taste. Bring slowly to the boil and cook for about 15 minutes, or until the sweet potatoes are tender. Add the fresh coriander, stir and adjust the seasoning if necessary. Serve at once.

AUBERGINE AND BASIL PARCELS

These are delicious little Italian bundles of tomatoes, mozzarella cheese and basil leaves, all wrapped up in generous slices of aubergine, served with a tomato dressing and nutty garnish.

Serves 4

2 large long aubergines
225g/8oz mozzarella cheese
2 plum tomatoes
16 large fresh basil leaves
30ml/2 tbsp olive oil
salt and ground black pepper
toasted pine nuts and torn basil leaves, to garnish

For the tomato dressing

60ml/4 tbsp olive oil
5ml/1 tsp balsamic vinegar
15ml/1 tbsp sun-dried tomato paste
15ml/1 tbsp lemon juice

Remove the stalks from the aubergines and cut the aubergines lengthways into thin slices. Bring a large saucepan of lightly salted water to the boil and cook the aubergine slices for about 2 minutes, until just softened. Drain, then dry on kitchen paper.

Cut the mozzarella cheese into eight slices. Cut each tomato into eight slices, not counting the first and last slices.

Take two aubergine slices and arrange one on top of the other in the form of a cross. Place a slice of tomato in the centre, season with salt and pepper, then add a basil leaf, followed by a slice of mozzarella, another basil leaf, a slice of tomato and more seasoning. Fold the ends of the aubergine slices around the mozzarella and tomato filling to make a neat parcel. Repeat with the rest of the assembled ingredients to make eight parcels. Place the parcels on a baking sheet and chill for about 20 minutes.

Make the tomato dressing. Whisk the olive oil, vinegar, sun-dried tomato paste and lemon juice in a bowl. Season to taste.

Preheat the grill. Brush the parcels with olive oil and grill for 5 minutes on each side until golden. Serve hot, with the dressing, sprinkled with pine nuts and basil leaves.

IMAM BAYILDI

This classic aubergine dish is accented with both ground and fresh coriander. According to legend, Imam Bayildi means "the Imam fainted", because he was so overcome by this delicious dish.

Serves 4

2 aubergines, halved lengthways
60ml/4 tbsp olive oil, plus extra if needed
2 large onions, thinly sliced
2 garlic cloves, crushed
1 green pepper, seeded and sliced
400g/14oz can chopped tomatoes
45ml/3 tbsp granulated sugar
5ml/1 tsp ground coriander
30ml/2 tbsp fresh chopped coriander
salt and ground black pepper
crusty bread, to serve
coriander sprigs, to serve

COOK'S TIP

Imam Bayildi can be served hot. It needs no accompaniment other than a bowl of Greek-style yogurt and some crusty bread or naan.

Using a sharp knife, slash the flesh of the aubergines a few times. Place them in a colander, sprinkle the cut sides with salt and leave for about 30 minutes. Rinse well and pat dry.

Preheat the oven to 190°C/375°F/Gas 5. Heat the oil in a frying pan, add the aubergines, cut-sides down, and fry for 5 minutes. Remove with a slotted spoon or tongs and place in a shallow ovenproof dish. Add the onions, garlic and green pepper to the pan, with extra oil if necessary, and cook for about 10 minutes, until the vegetables have softened. Add the tomatoes, sugar and ground coriander with salt and pepper to taste. Cook for about 5 minutes until the mixture has reduced. Stir in the chopped coriander.

Spoon this mixture on top of the aubergines. Cover and bake for about 30–35 minutes. Cool, then chill. Serve cold with crusty bread, garnished with coriander sprigs.

NUT AND CORIANDER PILAFF

Ground coriander adds fragrance to basmati rice in this perfect pilaff.

Serves 4–6

225g/8oz/1 cup basmati rice
15–30ml/1–2 tbsp sunflower oil
1 onion, chopped
1 garlic clove, crushed
1 large carrot, coarsely grated
5ml/1 tsp cumin seeds
10ml/2 tsp black mustard seeds (optional)
10ml/2 tsp ground coriander
4 cardamom pods
475ml/16fl oz/2 cups vegetable stock or water
1 bay leaf
75g/3oz/¾ cup unsalted nuts
salt and ground black pepper
fresh chopped coriander, to garnish

Put the rice into a large bowl of cold water. Swill the grains around with your hands, then tip out the cloudy water. Repeat this action about five times. If there is time, soak the rice for 30 minutes, then drain well in a sieve.

Heat the oil in a large shallow pan. Fry the onion, garlic and carrot over a gentle heat for a few minutes, then stir in the rice, seeds and spices. Cook for about 1–2 minutes, stirring, so that the grains are all coated in the oil.

Pour in the stock, add the bay leaf and season well. Bring to the boil, lower the heat, cover and simmer gently for 10 minutes. Without lifting the lid, remove the pan from the heat and leave for 5 minutes; this helps the rice to firm up and finish cooking. When the rice is fully cooked, there will be small steam holes in the centre. Discard the bay leaf and cardamom pods.

Stir in the nuts and check the seasoning. Scatter the chopped coriander over the pilaff and serve at once.

TOMATO RISOTTO WITH BASIL

Use plum tomatoes in this dish. Their fresh vibrant flavour is the perfect foil for the basil.

Serves 4

675g/1½lb firm ripe tomatoes, preferably plum tomatoes
50g/2oz/4 tbsp butter
1 onion, finely chopped
about 1.2 litres/2 pints/5 cups vegetable stock
275g/10oz/1½ cups arborio rice
400g/14oz can cannellini beans, drained
50g/2oz/⅔ cup grated Parmesan cheese, plus extra to garnish
salt and ground black pepper
10–12 fresh basil leaves, to garnish

COOK'S TIP
Shave the Parmesan by using a swivel-bladed potato peeler.

Cut the tomatoes in half and scoop out the seeds into a sieve placed over a bowl. Press the seeds with a spoon to extract all the juice. Set aside. Grill the tomatoes skin-side up until the skins are blackened. Rub off the skins and dice the flesh.

Melt the butter in a large pan, add the onion and cook for 5 minutes. Add the tomatoes with the reserved juice. Season, then cook for 10 minutes.

Meanwhile, bring the vegetable stock to the boil in another pan.

Add the rice to the tomato mixture and stir to coat. Add a ladleful of the stock and stir gently until absorbed. Repeat, adding a ladleful of stock at a time, until all the stock is absorbed and the rice is tender and creamy. Stir in the beans and Parmesan and heat through for a few minutes. Serve, sprinkling each portion with shredded basil leaves and grated Parmesan.

GNOCCHI WITH PARSLEY SAUCE

A mushroom and parsley sauce brings an exquisite flavour to these Italian potato dumplings.

Serves 4

450g/1lb peeled floury potatoes
450g/1lb peeled pumpkin, chopped
2 egg yolks
about 200g/7oz/1¾ cups plain flour
pinch of ground allspice
1.5ml/¼ tsp ground cinnamon
pinch of grated nutmeg
finely grated rind of ½ orange
50g/2oz/⅔ cup Parmesan cheese, shaved
salt and freshly ground black pepper

For the sauce

30ml/2 tbsp olive oil
1 shallot
175g/6oz fresh chanterelles or oyster mushrooms, sliced
10ml/2 tsp butter
150ml/¼ pint/⅔ cup crème fraîche
a little milk or water
75ml/5 tbsp chopped fresh parsley

Cook the potatoes in simmering salted water for about 20 minutes until tender. Drain and set aside. Place the pumpkin in a bowl, cover and microwave on full power for 8 minutes. Alternatively, wrap the pumpkin in foil and bake at 180°C/350°F/Gas 4 for 30 minutes. Drain well, add to the potatoes and then pass through a vegetable mill into a bowl. Add the egg yolks, flour, spices, orange rind and seasoning and mix to make a soft dough, adding more flour if the mixture is too soft.

Bring a large pan of salted water to the boil and dredge a work surface with plain flour. Spoon the gnocchi mixture into a piping bag fitted with a 1cm/½in plain nozzle. Pipe on to the floured surface to make a 15cm/6in sausage. Roll in flour and cut into 2.5cm/1in pieces. Repeat the process, making more sausage shapes. Mark each lightly with a fork and cook for 3–4 minutes in the boiling water. If cooking in batches, keep the gnocchi warm in a covered dish while cooking the remainder.

Make the sauce. Heat the oil in a non-stick frying pan and fry the shallot until softened but not browned. Add the mushrooms, cook briefly and then add the butter. Stir to melt and stir in the crème fraîche. Simmer briefly and adjust the consistency with milk or water. Add the parsley and season to taste with salt and pepper.

Lift the gnocchi out of the water with a slotted spoon and place in warmed soup bowls. Spoon the sauce over the top and scatter with Parmesan cheese shavings.

Vegetable Cannelloni with Rosemary

A subtle hint of rosemary enhances this milk-flavoured pasta dish, evoking a Mediterranean mood.

Serves 4–6

1 onion, finely chopped
2 garlic cloves, crushed
2 carrots, coarsely grated
2 celery sticks, finely chopped
150ml/¼ pint/⅔ cup vegetable stock
115g/4oz red or green lentils
400g/14oz can chopped tomatoes
30ml/2 tbsp tomato purée
2.5ml/½ tsp ground ginger
5ml/1 tsp chopped fresh rosemary
5ml/1 tsp chopped fresh thyme
40g/1½oz/3 tbsp butter
40g/1½oz/generous 1 tbsp plain flour
600ml/1 pint/2½ cups milk
1 bay leaf
large pinch of grated nutmeg
16–18 cannelloni
25g/1oz Cheddar cheese, grated
25g/1oz Parmesan cheese, grated
25g/1oz fresh white breadcrumbs
salt and ground black pepper
flat leaf parsley, to garnish

To make the filling, put the onion, garlic, carrots and celery into a large saucepan, add half the stock, cover and cook for 5 minutes or until the vegetables are tender.

Add the lentils, chopped tomatoes, tomato purée, ginger, rosemary, thyme and seasoning. Bring to the boil, cover and cook for 20 minutes. Remove the lid and cook for a further 10 minutes until thick and soft. Set aside to cool.

To make the sauce, put the butter, flour, milk and bay leaf into a pan and whisk over the heat until thick and smooth. Season with salt, pepper and nutmeg. Discard the bay leaf.

Fill the uncooked cannelloni by piping the filling into each tube. (It is easiest to hold them upright with one end flat on a board, while piping into the other end.)

Preheat the oven to 180°C/350°F/Gas 4. Spoon half the sauce into the bottom of a 20cm/8in square ovenproof dish. Lay 2 rows of filled cannelloni on top and spoon over the remaining sauce. Scatter over the cheeses and breadcrumbs. Bake in the oven for 30–40 minutes. Grill to brown the top, if necessary. Garnish with flat leaf parsley before serving.

Ricotta and Basil Tart

Rich and creamy, this basil-scented tart makes the perfect centrepiece for a summer buffet.

Serves 8–10

150g/5oz/1¼ cups plain flour
2.5ml/½ tsp salt
75g/3oz/6 tbsp butter
75g/3oz/6 tbsp margarine

For the filling

50g/2oz/2 cups basil leaves
25g/1oz/1 cup flat leaf parsley
120ml/4fl oz/½ cup extra virgin olive oil
2 eggs, beaten, plus 1 egg yolk
800g/1¾ lb/3½ cups ricotta cheese
50g/2oz/½ cup black olives, stoned
50g/2oz/½ cup grated Parmesan cheese
salt and ground black pepper

Combine the flour and salt in a bowl. Rub in the butter and margarine until the mixture resembles coarse breadcrumbs. Stir in just enough iced water to bind the dough. Gather into a ball, wrap and chill for at least 20 minutes.

Preheat the oven to 190°C/375°F/Gas 5. Roll out the dough thinly and line a 25cm/10in tart tin. Prick the base, then bake blind for 12 minutes. Remove the paper and weights and bake for about 3–5 minutes until golden. Turn the heat down to 180°C/350°F/Gas 4.

Mix the basil, parsley and olive oil in a food processor or blender. Season well with salt and pepper and process until finely chopped.

Whisk the eggs and yolk, gently fold in the ricotta, then fold in the basil mixture and olives. Stir in the Parmesan and adjust the seasoning. Pour the filling into the pastry case and bake for 30–35 minutes until set. Serve warm.

Courgette and Basil Quiche

If possible, use a hard goat's cheese for this flan as its flavour complements the courgettes and basil.

Serves 6

115g/4oz/scant 1 cup wholemeal flour

115g/4oz/1 cup plain flour

115g/4oz/½ cup butter or margarine

For the filling

30ml/2 tbsp olive oil

1 red onion, thinly sliced

2 large courgettes, sliced

175g/6oz/1½ cups grated cheese

30ml/2 tbsp shredded fresh basil

3 eggs, beaten

300ml/½ pint/1¼ cups milk

salt and ground black pepper

COOK'S TIP

To bake blind, line the pastry case with greaseproof paper and fill it with baking beans. Bake for the time specified, removing paper and beans for the final 5 minutes to crisp the base.

Preheat the oven to 200°C/400°F/Gas 6. Mix the flours together in a large bowl. Rub in the butter or margarine until the mixture resembles breadcrumbs, then mix to a firm dough with cold water. Roll out the pastry and use it to line a 23–25cm/9–10in flan tin. Prick the base, chill for 30 minutes, then bake blind for 20 minutes. Remove the flan case from the oven. Turn the heat down to 180°C/350°F/Gas 4.

Heat the oil in a frying pan and sweat the onion for 5 minutes until soft. Add the courgettes and fry for 5 minutes. Spoon the onion and courgettes into the pastry case. Scatter over most of the cheese and all of the basil.

Beat the eggs and milk with salt and pepper to taste. Pour over the filling. Top with the remaining cheese. Bake the flan for about 40 minutes, or until risen and just firm to the touch in the centre. Cool slightly before serving.

Vegetable Pizza with Basil

Use any combination of colourful fresh vegetables on this scrumptious pizza. A sizzling golden mozzarella and basil topping ensures it's a big hit with the whole family.

Serves 4

400g/14oz can peeled plum tomatoes, drained
2 broccoli spears
225g/8oz fresh asparagus spears
2 small courgettes
75ml/5 tbsp olive oil
50g/2oz/½ cup frozen peas, thawed
4 spring onions, sliced
28cm/11in ready-to-bake pizza base, homemade or bought
75g/3oz/½ cup mozzarella cheese, cut into small dice
10 fresh basil leaves, torn in pieces
2 garlic cloves, finely chopped
salt and ground black pepper

Preheat the oven to 240°C/475°F/Gas 9 for at least 20 minutes before baking the pizza. Purée the tomatoes in a blender or food processor, or press them through a strainer into a bowl.

Peel the broccoli stems and asparagus. Bring a saucepan of water to the boil, add the broccoli, asparagus and courgettes and boil for 4–5 minutes. Drain and cut the vegetables into bite-size pieces.

Heat 30ml/2 tbsp of the olive oil in a small saucepan. Stir in the thawed peas and spring onions, and cook for 5–6 minutes, stirring frequently. Remove from the heat.

Spread the puréed tomatoes on the pizza dough, leaving the rim uncovered. Add the blanched and sautéed vegetables, arranging them neatly and evenly over the tomatoes.

Sprinkle with the mozzarella, basil, garlic, salt and pepper, and drizzle with the remaining olive oil. Bake for about 20 minutes, or until the crust is golden brown and the cheese has melted.

POTATO, ROSEMARY AND GARLIC PIZZA

New potatoes, smoked mozzarella, rosemary and garlic make the flavour of this pizza unique.

Serves 2–3

350g/12oz new potatoes
45ml/3 tbsp olive oil
2 garlic cloves, crushed
1 pizza base, 25–30cm/10–12in in diameter
1 red onion, thinly sliced
150g/5oz smoked mozzarella cheese, grated
10ml/2 tsp chopped fresh rosemary
salt and ground black pepper
30ml/2 tbsp freshly grated Parmesan cheese, to garnish

Preheat the oven to 220°C/425°F/Gas 7. Cook the potatoes in boiling salted water for 5 minutes. Drain well. When cool, peel and slice thinly.

Heat 30ml/2 tbsp of the oil in a frying-pan. Add the sliced potatoes and garlic and fry for 5–8 minutes until the potatoes are tender.

Brush the pizza base with the remaining oil. Scatter over the onion, then arrange the potatoes on top. Sprinkle with the mozzarella and rosemary. Grind over plenty of black pepper and bake in the oven for 15–20 minutes until crisp and golden. Remove from the oven and sprinkle with the Parmesan before serving.

fish and seafood dishes

If you need to provide a nutritious, tasty meal in scarcely any time at all, opt for fish or seafood, enhanced with the freshest herbs. Try Minted Sea Bream or Parsley-stuffed Plaice Rolls, Coriander-coated Prawns or Halibut with Basil Salsa, to name just a few of the fabulous dishes that follow.

ROSEMARY MULLET IN BANANA LEAVES

The exceptionally sweet and rich flavour of red mullet is enhanced by the aroma of rosemary, and banana leaves help to seal in the juices of this firm-textured fish.

Serves 4

8 small red mullet or kingfish, about 175g/6oz each

8 fresh rosemary sprigs, plus extra to garnish

banana leaves or wax paper

30ml/2 tbsp olive oil

salt and ground black pepper

COOK'S TIP

There are two varieties of red mullet available. The best is actually called golden mullet.

Preheat the oven to 220°C/425°F/Gas 7.

Wash, scale and gut the fish or ask your fishmonger to do this for you. Lay a rosemary sprig inside the cavity of each fish. Cut a piece of banana leaf or a sheet of wax paper large enough to wrap each fish.

Drizzle the mullet with a little olive oil and season well. Wrap each fish securely in the banana leaves or wax paper. Place the parcels on a baking sheet, seam side down. Bake in the oven for about 12 minutes, until cooked through and tender. Unwrap the parcels to serve and garnish with more fresh rosemary sprigs.

ROSEMARY BAKED FISH

This North African dish, evoking all the colour and rich tastes of Mediterranean cuisine, is served with an unusual and delicious rosemary-flavoured sauce.

Serves 4

1 whole white fish, about 1.1kg/2½lb, scaled and cleaned
10ml/2 tsp coriander seeds
4 garlic cloves, sliced
10ml/2 tsp harissa sauce
90ml/6 tbsp olive oil
6 plum tomatoes, sliced
1 mild onion, sliced
3 preserved lemons or 1 fresh lemon
plenty of fresh herbs, such as rosemary, bay leaves and thyme
salt and ground black pepper
extra fresh herbs, to garnish

For the sauce

75ml/3fl oz/⅓ cup light tahini
juice of 1 lemon
1 garlic clove, crushed
45ml/3 tbsp finely chopped fresh rosemary

Preheat the oven to 200°C/400°F/Gas 6. Grease the base and sides of a large shallow ovenproof dish or roasting tin.

Slash the fish diagonally on both sides with a sharp knife. Finely crush the coriander seeds and garlic using a pestle and mortar. Mix with the harissa sauce and about 60ml/4 tbsp of the olive oil.

Spread a little of the harissa, coriander and garlic paste inside the cavity of the fish. Spread the remainder over each side of the fish and set aside.

Scatter the tomatoes, onion and preserved or fresh lemon into the prepared dish or tin. (Thinly slice the lemon if using a fresh one). Sprinkle with the remaining oil and season with salt and pepper. Lay the fish on top and tuck plenty of rosemary and other herbs around it. Bake in the oven uncovered, for about 25 minutes, or until the fish has turned opaque – test by piercing the thickest part with a knife.

Meanwhile, make the sauce. Put the tahini, lemon juice, garlic and rosemary in a small saucepan with 120ml/4fl oz/½ cup water and add a little salt and pepper. Cook gently until smooth and heated through. Serve in a separate dish, alongside the baked fish.

MINTED SEA BREAM

Pine nuts, raisins and cinnamon mingle with mint in this Middle Eastern dish.

Serves 4

1.75kg/4lb whole sea bream or 2 smaller sea bream
30ml/2 tbsp olive oil
75g/3oz/¾ cup pine nuts
1 large onion, finely chopped
450g/1lb ripe tomatoes, roughly chopped
75g/3oz/½ cup raisins
1.5ml/¼ tsp ground cinnamon
1.5ml/¼ tsp ground mixed spice
45ml/3 tbsp chopped fresh mint
225g/8oz/1 cup long-grain rice
3 lemon slices
300ml/½ pint/1¼ cups fish stock
salt

COOK'S TIP

Sea bream is a large family of fish and all varieties are equally delicious. Black and red sea bream and daurade are the most readily available.

Trim, gut and scale the fish or ask your fishmonger to do this for you. Preheat the oven to 180°C/350°F/Gas 4.

Heat the oil in a large, heavy-based saucepan and stir-fry the pine nuts for 1 minute. Add the onion and continue to stir-fry until it is soft but not coloured. Add the tomatoes and simmer for 10 minutes.

Stir in the raisins, most of the cinnamon and mixed spice, the mint, rice and lemon slices. Transfer the mixture to a large roasting tin and pour over the stock. Arrange the fish on top and cut several diagonal slashes in the skin with a sharp knife. Sprinkle over a little salt, the remaining cinnamon and mixed spice and bake in the oven for 30–35 minutes for the large fish or 20–25 minutes for the smaller fish.

SPICED MINT RAINBOW TROUT

Rainbow trout fillets coated in a minty marinade make a tasty quick meal cooked on a grill or barbecue.

Serves 4

4 large rainbow trout fillets, about 150g/5oz each
15ml/1 tbsp ground coriander
1 garlic clove, crushed
30ml/2 tbsp finely chopped fresh mint
5ml/1 tsp paprika
175ml/6fl oz/¾ cup natural yogurt
salad and pitta bread, to serve

With a sharp knife, slash the flesh of the fish fillets through the skin fairly deeply at intervals.

Mix together the coriander, garlic, mint, paprika and yogurt. Spread this mixture evenly over the fish and leave to marinate for about an hour.

Cook the fish under a preheated moderately hot grill or on a barbecue, turning occasionally, until crisp and golden. Serve hot with a crisp salad and some warmed pitta bread.

Nowadays, rainbow trout are mainly farmed fish and extra flavouring is usually essential to bring out the best in them. However, the delicious combination of coriander, mint and yogurt would also suit the more delicate flavour of brown trout, if you are lucky enough to find them. In this case, garlic may be too robust and is probably better omitted.

COOK'S TIP

If you are using the grill rather than the barbecue, it is best to line the grill pan with foil before cooking the trout.

TROUT WITH MUSHROOM SAUCE

The subtle flavour of trout is enhanced by this creamy mushroom sauce.

Serves 4

8 pink trout fillets
seasoned plain flour, for dusting
75g/3oz/6 tbsp butter
1 garlic clove, chopped
10ml/2 tsp chopped fresh sage
350g/12oz assorted mushrooms, such as button, chestnut and oyster, trimmed and sliced
90ml/6 tbsp dry white wine
250ml/8fl oz/1 cup double cream
salt and ground black pepper
sage sprigs, to garnish

Remove the skin from the trout fillets, then carefully remove any bones. Lightly dust the trout fillets on both sides in the seasoned flour, shaking off any excess.

Melt the butter in a large frying pan, add the trout fillets and fry gently over a moderate heat for 4–5 minutes, turning once. Remove from the pan and keep warm. Add the chopped garlic, sage and mushrooms to the pan and gently fry until softened.

Pour in the wine and boil briskly to allow the alcohol to evaporate. Stir in the cream and season to taste with salt and pepper.

Serve the trout fillets on warmed plates with the sauce spooned over. Garnish with a few sage sprigs.

COOK'S TIP

Use a large sharp knife to ease the skin from the trout fillets, then pull out any bones from the flesh – a pair of tweezers makes easy work of this fiddly task!

Dover Sole in a Parsley Jacket

Quick to prepare and absolutely delicious, there is nothing to compare with the rich sweetness of Dover sole. The parsley adds a subtle flavour as well as looking magnificent.

Serves 2

2 Dover sole, skinned
25g/1oz/2 tbsp butter
salt and freshly ground black pepper
lemon wedges, halved cherry tomatoes and fresh flat leaf parsley sprigs, to garnish
mashed potatoes, to serve

For the parsley jacket

25g/1oz fresh flat leaf parsley
25g/1oz crustless white bread, cubed
45ml/3 tbsp milk
30ml/2 tbsp olive oil
finely grated rind of ½ small lemon
2 small garlic cloves, crushed

First make the parsley jacket. Place the parsley in a food processor and process until finely chopped. Add the bread, milk, olive oil, lemon rind and garlic and process to make a fine paste.

Preheat a moderate grill. Season the fish, dot with butter and grill for 5 minutes. Turn and grill for 2 minutes on the other side. Spread this side with the parsley mixture and cook under the grill for a further 5 minutes until the fish flakes easily. Garnish the fish with lemon wedges, tomato halves and parsley and serve with creamy mashed potatoes.

Spanish-style Hake with Parsley

This is essentially a main meal soup. Fish, mussels and green beans make the substance of the soup while the stock is flavoured with wine, sherry and lots of lovely parsley.

Serves 4

16–20 fresh mussels
30ml/2 tbsp olive oil
25g/1oz/2 tbsp butter
1 onion, chopped
3 garlic cloves, crushed
15ml/1 tbsp plain flour
2.5ml/½ tsp paprika
4 hake cutlets, about 175g/6oz each
225g/8oz fine green beans, cut into 2.5cm/1in lengths
350ml/12fl oz/1½ cups fish stock
150ml/¼ pint/⅔ cup dry white wine
30ml/2 tbsp dry sherry
45ml/3 tbsp chopped fresh parsley
salt and freshly ground black pepper
crusty bread, to serve

Scrub the mussels thoroughly, pulling away the gritty beards. Discard any mussels that don't close when sharply tapped with a knife. Heat the oil and butter in a frying pan and fry the onion for 5 minutes until softened but not browned. Add the crushed garlic and cook for a further 1 minute.

Mix together the flour and paprika and lightly dust the hake cutlets. Push the onion and garlic to one side of the pan and add the fish. Fry on both sides until golden, then carefully stir in the beans, stock, wine, sherry and seasoning. Bring to the boil and cook for about 2 minutes.

Add the prepared mussels and parsley, cover the pan and cook for 5–8 minutes until the mussels have opened. Discard any mussels that remain closed.

Serve this dish in warmed, shallow soup bowls with crusty bread to mop up the juices.

COOK'S TIP

Cod and haddock cutlets will work just as well in this tasty dish.

HALIBUT WITH BASIL SALSA

Freshly grilled halibut fillets served with a tangy tomato and basil salsa make a perfect summertime dinner. Just sit back and let your tastebuds enjoy the treat.

Serves 4

4 halibut fillets, about 175g/6oz each, skinned
45ml/3 tbsp olive oil
salt and ground black pepper

For the salsa

1 tomato, roughly chopped
¼ red onion, finely chopped
1 small drained canned jalapeño chilli
30ml/2 tbsp balsamic vinegar
10 large fresh basil leaves
15ml/1 tbsp olive oil

COOK'S TIP

This is delicious barbecued. Cook it in a hinged grill and take care when basting as olive oil dripped on to the coals will cause flare-ups.

Make the salsa. Mix the tomato, red onion, jalapeño chilli and balsamic vinegar in a bowl.

Shred the basil leaves finely, and stir them into the tomato salsa, with the olive oil. Add salt and pepper to taste. Cover and leave to marinate for at least 3 hours.

Rub the halibut fillets with olive oil, salt and pepper. Preheat the grill. Cook the halibut for about 4 minutes on each side, depending on the thickness. Baste with olive oil as necessary. Serve with the salsa.

HADDOCK AND PARSLEY SAUCE

Parsley sauce is a classic with white fish but it is excellent with smoked fish too. Add lots of parsley and season well so that the sauce stands up to the smoky flavour of the fish.

Serves 4

4 smoked haddock fillets, about 225g/8oz each
75g/3oz/6 tbsp butter, softened
25g/1oz/2 tbsp plain flour
300ml/½ pint/1¼ cups milk
60ml/4 tbsp chopped fresh parsley
salt and freshly ground black pepper
fresh parsley sprigs, to garnish

Smear the fish fillets on both sides with 50g/2oz/4 tbsp of the butter and preheat the grill. Beat the remaining butter and flour together to make a thick paste.

Grill the fish for 10–15 minutes, turning when necessary. Meanwhile, heat the milk until just below boiling point. Add the flour mixture in small pieces, whisking constantly over the heat. Continue until you have used all the flour mixture and the sauce is smooth and thick.

Stir in the parsley and season well to taste. Pour over the fish, garnish with parsley and serve.

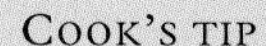

COOK'S TIP

You could use flat leaf or curly parsley for this dish. Flat leaf parsley has the more aromatic flavour but curly parsley is also very good and would be the traditional variety to serve with this British dish.

Pan-Fried Red Mullet with Basil and Citrus Fruits

Red mullet is popular throughout the Mediterranean and this Italian recipe combines it with anchovies, oranges, lemons and basil for an unusual taste sensation.

Serves 4

4 red mullet, about 225g/8oz each, filleted
90ml/6 tbsp olive oil
10 peppercorns, crushed
2 oranges, 1 peeled and sliced and 1 squeezed
1 lemon
15g/½oz/2 tbsp plain flour
15g/½oz/1 tbsp butter
2 drained canned anchovies, chopped
60ml/4 tbsp shredded fresh basil
salt and ground black pepper

Place the fish fillets in a single layer in a shallow dish. Pour over the olive oil and sprinkle with the crushed peppercorns. Lay the orange slices on top of the fish. Cover the dish, and leave it to marinate in the fridge for at least 4 hours.

Cut the lemon in half. Remove the skin and pith from one half using a small sharp knife, and slice thinly. Squeeze the juice from the other half.

Lift the fish out of the marinade, and pat dry on kitchen paper. Reserve the marinade and orange slices. Season the fish with salt and pepper and dust lightly with flour.

Heat 45ml/3 tbsp of the reserved marinade in a large frying pan. Add the fish and fry for 2 minutes on each side. Remove from the pan and keep hot. Discard the marinade that is left in the pan.

Melt the butter in the pan with the remaining original marinade. Add the anchovies and cook until they begin to disintegrate. Stir in the orange and lemon juice, then check the seasoning and simmer until slightly reduced. Stir in the basil. Pour the sauce over the fish and garnish with the reserved orange and lemon slices.

Cook's Tip

If you prefer, use other fish fillets for this dish, such as lemon sole, haddock or hake.

PARSLEY-STUFFED PLAICE ROLLS

Sun-dried tomatoes, pine nuts and plenty of flat leaf parsley make an appetizing stuffing with a superb southern European flavour.

Serves 4

4 plaice fillets, about 225g/8oz each, skinned
75g/3oz/6 tbsp butter
1 small onion, chopped
1 celery stick, finely chopped
115g/4oz/2 cups fresh white breadcrumbs
45ml/3 tbsp chopped fresh flat leaf parsley
30ml/2 tbsp pine nuts, toasted
3–4 sun-dried tomatoes in oil, drained and chopped
50g/2oz can anchovy fillets, drained and chopped
75ml/5 tbsp hot fish stock
freshly ground black pepper

COOK'S TIP

This dish is superb served with baby new potatoes topped with a knob of butter.

Preheat the oven to 180°C/350°F/Gas 4. Using a sharp knife, cut the plaice fillets in half lengthways to make eight smaller fillets. Melt the butter in a pan. Add the onion and celery and cook, covered, over a very gentle heat for about 15 minutes until they are both very soft. Mix together the breadcrumbs, parsley, pine nuts, sun-dried tomatoes and anchovies in a bowl. Stir in the softened vegetables and buttery juices and season with freshly ground black pepper.

Divide the stuffing into eight portions and form each one into a small ball. Roll this up inside a plaice fillet, securing each roll with a cocktail stick.

Place the rolled-up fillets in a buttered ovenproof dish. Pour over the fish stock, cover with buttered foil and bake for about 20 minutes until the fish flakes easily. Remove the cocktail sticks and serve with a little of the cooking juices drizzled over.

Salmon with Sizzling Coriander

This superb salmon dish comes from America, where fresh coriander is known as "cilantro".

Serves 4

4 salmon steaks, about 175g/6oz each
60ml/4 tbsp chopped fresh coriander
45ml/3 tbsp grated fresh root ginger
3 spring onions, finely chopped
60ml/4 tbsp soy sauce, plus extra to serve
75ml/5 tbsp olive oil
salt and ground black pepper
lettuce and coriander sprigs, to garnish

Season the salmon steaks on both sides with salt and pepper. Prepare a steamer (see Cook's Tip), add the salmon steaks, cover and steam for 7–8 minutes until the fish is opaque throughout.

Place the steamed salmon steaks on warmed plates. Divide the chopped coriander among them, mounding it on top of the fish. Sprinkle with the ginger and then the spring onions. Drizzle 15ml/1 tbsp of soy sauce over each salmon steak. Heat the oil in a small heavy-based saucepan until very hot. Spoon the hot oil over each salmon steak and serve immediately, with more soy sauce, if you like. Garnish with lettuce and coriander sprigs.

Cook's Tip

If you do not own a steamer, cook the fish steaks on a lightly buttered plate over a pan of simmering water. Cover the fish with greaseproof paper or invert a second plate on top.

MINTY COD PLAKI

A wonderful Greek recipe in which cod is cooked gently in olive oil with onions and tomatoes flavoured with mint and other fresh aromatic herbs.

Serves 6

300ml/½ pint/1¼ cups olive oil
2 onions, thinly sliced
2 large well-flavoured tomatoes, roughly chopped
3 garlic cloves, thinly sliced
5ml/1 tsp sugar
5ml/1 tsp chopped fresh mint
5ml/1 tsp chopped fresh dill
5ml/1 tsp chopped fresh celery leaves
15ml/1 tbsp chopped fresh parsley
300ml/½ pint/1¼ cups water
6 cod steaks
juice of 1 lemon
salt and ground black pepper
sprigs of fresh mint, to garnish

Heat the oil in a large sauté pan or flameproof dish. Add the onions and cook until pale golden and softened. Add the tomatoes, garlic, sugar, mint, dill, celery leaves and parsley with the water. Season with salt and pepper, then simmer, uncovered, for 25 minutes, until the liquid has reduced by about one-third.

Add the fish steaks and cook gently for 10–12 minutes, until the fish is just cooked. Remove from the heat and add the lemon juice. Cover and leave to stand for about 20 minutes before serving. Arrange the cod in a dish and spoon the sauce over. Garnish with mint and serve warm or cold.

PLAICE AND PESTO PARCELS

Opening these parcels is pure pleasure as a heavenly aroma of basil and lemon escapes.

Serves 4

75g/3oz/6 tbsp butter

20ml/4 tsp homemade or bought pesto

8 small plaice fillets, skinned

1 small fennel bulb, cut into matchsticks

2 small carrots, cut into matchsticks

2 courgettes, cut into matchsticks

10ml/2 tsp finely grated lemon rind

vegetable oil, for brushing

salt and ground black pepper

fresh basil leaves, to garnish

Preheat the oven to 190°C/375°F/Gas 5. Beat three-quarters of the butter with the pesto and season to taste. Spread the pesto butter over the skinned side of each plaice fillet and roll up from the thick end.

Melt the remaining butter in a small saucepan, add the fennel and carrots and sauté for 3 minutes. Add the courgettes and cook for 2 minutes. Remove from the heat and add the lemon rind, with salt and pepper to taste.

Cut four squares of greaseproof paper, each large enough to enclose two plaice rolls. Brush with oil. Spoon a quarter of the vegetables into the centre of each, then arrange two plaice rolls on top. Seal the parcels tightly and place in a roasting tin. Bake for 15–20 minutes, until the fish is just tender.

To serve, open the parcels, sprinkle with the basil leaves and grind over a little black pepper.

COOK'S TIP

Take the parcels hot from the oven to the table – the greaseproof paper becomes translucent when baked and looks very attractive.

Baked Tuna with Coriander Crust

There's nothing like a fresh coriander marinade to liven up the flavour of meaty fresh tuna steaks.

Serves 4

finely grated rind of 1 lemon
5ml/1 tsp black peppercorns
½ small onion, finely chopped
30ml/2 tbsp chopped fresh coriander
4 fresh tuna steaks, about 175g/6oz each
120ml/4fl oz/½ cup olive oil

For the salsa

1 mango, peeled and diced
finely grated rind and juice of 1 lime
½ fresh red chilli, seeded and finely chopped

Make the salsa. Mix the mango, lime rind and juice and chilli in a bowl and leave to marinate for at least 1 hour.

Grind the lemon rind, black peppercorns, onion and coriander to a coarse paste, using a mortar and pestle or a coffee grinder. Spoon a quarter of the mixture on to one side of each tuna steak, pressing on well.

Heat the olive oil in a heavy-based frying pan until it begins to smoke. Add the tuna, paste-side down, and fry until a crust forms. Lower the heat and turn the steaks to cook for 1 minute more. Pat off any excess oil with kitchen paper and serve with the salsa.

Cook's Tip

Tuna is an excellent choice for the barbecue. Cook the steaks in a hinged grill over moderately hot coals.

Fish Kebabs with Coriander

Skewers of fresh fish and vegetables basted in a coriander marinade make irresistible kebabs.

Serves 4

275g/10oz cod fillets, or any other firm white fish fillets, skinned
45ml/3 tbsp lemon juice
5ml/1 tsp grated fresh root ginger
2 fresh green chillies, finely chopped
15ml/1 tbsp finely chopped fresh coriander
15ml/1 tbsp finely chopped fresh mint
5ml/1 tsp ground coriander
5ml/1 tsp salt
1 red pepper
1 green pepper
½ cauliflower
8–10 button mushrooms
8 cherry tomatoes
15ml/1 tbsp soya oil
saffron rice, to serve

Cut the fish fillets into large chunks. Mix the lemon juice, ginger, chillies, fresh coriander, mint, ground coriander and salt in a mixing bowl. Add the fish chunks, mix to coat and marinate for about 30 minutes.

Cut the red and green peppers into large squares, discarding the core and seeds from each. Divide the cauliflower into individual florets. Preheat the grill.

Thread the peppers, cauliflower florets, mushrooms and cherry tomatoes alternately with the fish pieces on to four skewers. Brush the kebabs with the oil and any remaining marinade. Transfer to a flameproof dish and grill for 7–10 minutes, or until the fish is opaque throughout. Serve on a bed of saffron rice.

SALMON PIE WITH LEMON THYME

This exceptional pie is highly recommended and uses salmon's special flavour to the full.

Serves 4–6

800g/1¾ lb salmon
45ml/3 tbsp walnut oil
15ml/1 tbsp lime juice
10ml/2 tsp chopped lemon thyme
30ml/2 tbsp white wine
salt and pepper
400g/14 oz puff pastry
50g/2 oz/½ cup flaked almonds
3–4 pieces stem ginger in syrup, chopped
1 egg, beaten
lemon thyme, to garnish

Split the salmon in half, remove all the bones and skin, and divide into four fillets. Mix the oil, lime juice, thyme, wine and pepper, and pour over the fish. Leave to marinate overnight in the fridge.

Divide the pastry into two pieces, one slightly larger than the other, and roll out – the smaller piece should be large enough to take two of the salmon fillets and the second piece about 5 cm/2 in larger all round. Drain the fillets. Discard the marinade.

Preheat the oven to 190°C/375°F/Gas 5. Place two of the fillets on the smaller piece of pastry, and season with the salt and pepper. Add the almonds and ginger and cover with the other two fillets.

Season again, cover with the second piece of pastry and seal well by brushing the edges of the pastry with water. Brush the top layer of pastry with beaten egg and decorate with any leftover pastry. Bake for 40 minutes. If the pastry starts to brown too much, cover with brown paper and continue to cook. Before serving, garnish with lemon thyme.

SEAFOOD RISOTTO WITH PARSLEY

Parsley and chervil add colour and a pleasant, aromatic flavour to this tasty risotto. Use short-grain Arborio rice which has a creamy texture to complement the shellfish and mushrooms.

Serves 4

225g/8oz fresh mussels
45ml/3 tbsp olive oil
1 onion, chopped
225g/8oz assorted wild and cultivated mushrooms, trimmed and sliced
450g/1lb/2¼ cups short-grain Arborio rice
1.2 litres/2 pints/5 cups boiling chicken or vegetable stock
150ml/¼ pint/⅔ cup white wine
115g/4oz raw prawns, peeled
225g/8oz clams
1 squid, cleaned, trimmed and sliced
75ml/5 tbsp mixed chopped fresh flat leaf parsley and chervil
celery salt and cayenne pepper

COOK'S TIP

Be sure to discard any uncooked mussels that do not close when sharply tapped.

Scrub the mussels thoroughly, pulling away the gritty beards. Discard any mussels that don't close when sharply tapped with a knife. Heat the oil in a large frying pan and fry the onion for 6–8 minutes until softened but not browned. Add the mushrooms and cook for 5–6 minutes, stirring occasionally. Add the rice and cook for about 1 minute to coat the rice in oil, then pour in the stock and wine. Add the prawns, mussels, clams and squid and simmer for 15 minutes, stirring occasionally. Discard any shellfish that have not opened during cooking.

Add the herbs, stir well, then remove from the heat. Cover tightly and allow to stand for 5–10 minutes until the rice is completely tender. Season with celery salt and cayenne pepper to taste, and serve.

CORIANDER-COATED PRAWNS

Taste sensations come thick and fast when you bite into one of these prawns. First, there is golden grilled cheese, then a crisp coriander crust and finally succulent shellfish.

Serves 4

75g/3oz/¾ cup cornflour
5–10ml/1–2 tsp cayenne pepper
2.5ml/½ tsp ground cumin
5ml/1 tsp salt
30ml/2 tbsp chopped fresh coriander
plain flour, for dredging
900g/2lb large raw prawns, peeled and deveined
60ml/4 tbsp vegetable oil
115g/4oz/1 cup grated mature Cheddar cheese
lime wedges and tomato salsa, to serve

Mix the cornflour, cayenne pepper, cumin, salt and coriander in a bowl. Have ready two shallow bowls, one holding water and the other the flour for dredging.

Coat the prawns lightly in flour, then dip in water and roll in the cornflour mixture to coat.

Heat the oil in a non-stick frying pan. When hot, add the prawns, in batches if necessary. Cook for 2–3 minutes on each side, until they are opaque. Drain on kitchen paper.

Place the prawns in a single layer in a large baking dish, or individual dishes. Sprinkle the cheese evenly over the top. Grill for 2–3 minutes, until the cheese melts. Serve immediately, with lime wedges and a tomato salsa.

COOK'S TIP

When preparing the prawns, remove the heads, but leave the tails intact.

CORIANDER CRAB WITH COCONUT

Coriander seeds add a pungent taste to this spicy dish – simply serve it with plain warm naan bread.

Serves 4

40g/1½ oz/½ cup dried unsweetened coconut flakes
2 garlic cloves, roughly chopped
5cm/2in piece of fresh root ginger, peeled and grated
2.5ml/½ tsp cumin seeds
1 small cinnamon stick, broken
2.5ml/½ tsp ground turmeric
2 dried red chillies, crumbled
15ml/1 tbsp coriander seeds
2.5ml/½ tsp poppy seeds
15ml/1 tbsp vegetable oil
1 onion, sliced
1 small green pepper, cut into strips
16 crab claws
fresh coriander sprigs, crushed, to garnish
150ml/¼ pint/⅔ cup natural yogurt, to serve

Place the dried coconut, garlic, ginger, cumin seeds, cinnamon, turmeric, chillies, and coriander and poppy seeds in a food processor or blender. Process until well blended.

Heat the oil in a wok and fry the onion until soft, but not coloured. Stir in the green pepper and stir-fry for 1 minute, then remove the vegetables with a slotted spoon. Set aside.

Heat the wok again. Add the crab claws, stir-fry for 2 minutes, then briefly return all the spiced vegetables to the wok. Toss over the heat for about 1 minute. Garnish with fresh coriander sprigs and serve with the cooling natural yogurt.

Crab Cakes with Parsley Sauce

These crab cakes are served with a tartar-like sauce, richly flavoured with onions, capers and parsley.

Serves 4

675g/1½lb fresh crab meat
1 egg, beaten
30ml/2 tbsp mayonnaise
15ml/1 tbsp Worcestershire sauce
15ml/1 tbsp dry sherry
30ml/2 tbsp finely chopped fresh parsley
15ml/1 tbsp finely chopped fresh chives or dill
45ml/3 tbsp olive oil
salt and freshly ground black pepper
chives, slices of lemon and salad leaves, to garnish

For the parsley sauce

1 egg yolk
15ml/1 tbsp white wine vinegar
30ml/2 tbsp Dijon mustard
250ml/8fl oz/1 cup sunflower oil
30ml/2 tbsp lemon juice
2 spring onions, finely chopped
30ml/2 tbsp drained capers, chopped
3–4 gherkins, finely chopped
45ml/3 tbsp chopped fresh parsley

Place the crab meat in a bowl, discarding any pieces of shell but keeping the pieces of crab as large as possible.

Put the egg, mayonnaise, Worcestershire sauce, sherry and chopped herbs in a bowl and stir to mix. Season with salt and pepper, then fold in the crab meat. Divide the mixture into eight oval cakes and place on a baking sheet between layers of greaseproof paper. Chill for at least 1 hour.

Meanwhile, make the sauce. Using a wire whisk, beat the egg yolk and add the vinegar, mustard and seasoning. Whisk in the oil, at first drop by drop and then in a slow, steady stream, to make a smooth mayonnaise. Add the lemon juice, spring onions, capers, gherkins and parsley and mix well. Adjust the seasoning, cover and chill.

Preheat the grill. Brush the crab cakes with the olive oil and place on an oiled baking sheet. Grill under a moderately hot heat for about 5 minutes each side until golden brown. Serve hot with the parsley sauce, garnished with chives, lemon slices and a few salad leaves.

poultry dishes

Mild-flavoured chicken and turkey marry well with most herbs, happily absorbing their flavours; a fact that is reflected in the variety of recipes in this section. These range from the more traditional, such as Chicken, Leek and Parsley Pie, to Chicken Liver Stir-fry with Rosemary and Turkey with Basil and Pepper Sauce.

Rosemary Pot-roast Poussins

Pot-roasting in the French manner ensures that poussins, which tend to be rather bland, absorb all the wonderful flavours of young vegetables and fresh rosemary.

Serves 4

15ml/1 tbsp olive oil
1 onion, sliced
1 large garlic clove, sliced
50g/2oz/½ cup diced lightly smoked bacon
2 poussins, about 625g/1¼lb each, or 4 small poussins, about 350g/12oz each
30ml/2 tbsp melted butter
2 baby celery hearts, each cut into 4
8 baby carrots
2 small courgettes, cut into chunks
8 small new potatoes
600ml/1 pint/2½ cups chicken stock
150ml/¼ pint/⅔ cup dry white wine
3 fresh rosemary sprigs
1 fresh thyme sprig
1 bay leaf
15ml/1 tbsp butter, softened
15ml/1 tbsp plain flour
salt and ground black pepper
fresh herbs, to garnish

Preheat the oven to 190°C/375°F/Gas 5. Heat the olive oil in a large flameproof casserole and add the onion, garlic and bacon. Sauté for 5–6 minutes until the onion has softened.

Brush the poussins with a little of the melted butter and season well. Lay on top of the onion mixture and arrange the prepared vegetables around them. Pour the chicken stock and wine around the birds and add the herbs.

Cover, bake in the oven for 20 minutes, then remove the lid and brush the birds with the remaining melted butter. Bake for a further 25–30 minutes until golden.

Transfer the poussins to a warmed serving platter. If using larger ones, cut them in half with poultry shears or scissors. Remove the vegetables from the casserole with a draining spoon and arrange them round the birds. Cover with foil and keep warm.

Discard the herbs from the cooking juices. In a bowl mix together the softened butter and flour to form a paste. Bring the liquid in the casserole to the boil and then whisk in teaspoonfuls of the paste until the sauce has thickened. Season the sauce and serve with the poussins and vegetables, garnished with fresh herbs.

CHICKEN WITH GARLIC AND ROSEMARY

A sweet wine and garlic sauce coats chicken gently scented with rosemary and thyme.

Serves 8

2kg/4½lb chicken pieces

30ml/2 tbsp olive oil

1 large onion, halved and sliced

3 large garlic bulbs, about 200g/7oz, separated into cloves and peeled

150ml/¼ pint/⅔ cup dry white wine

175ml/6fl oz/¾ cup chicken stock

4–5 fresh rosemary sprigs

2 fresh thyme sprigs

1 bay leaf

salt and ground black pepper

COOK'S TIP

Use fresh, new season's garlic if you can find it. There's no need to peel the cloves if the skin is not papery, just remove the outer layer. In France, the cooked garlic cloves are sometimes spread on toasted country bread.

Preheat the oven to 190°C/375°F/Gas 5. Pat the chicken pieces dry with kitchen paper and season with salt and pepper.

Heat the olive oil in a large flameproof casserole and add the chicken pieces in batches, skin side down. Brown over a medium-high heat, turning frequently. Transfer the chicken to a plate.

Add the onion and garlic to the casserole, cover and cook over a medium-low heat until lightly browned, stirring frequently.

Add the wine and bring to the boil; return the chicken to the casserole. Add the stock and herbs and bring back to the boil. Cover and transfer to the oven. Cook for 25 minutes or until the chicken is tender and the juices run clear when the thickest part of the thigh is pierced with a knife.

Remove the chicken pieces from the casserole and strain the cooking liquid. Discard the herbs, transfer the onion and garlic to a food processor and purée until smooth. Skim off any fat from the cooking liquid and discard. Return the cooking liquid to the casserole. Stir in the garlic and onion purée, return the chicken to the casserole and reheat gently for 3–4 minutes before serving.

MINTY YOGURT CHICKEN

The subtle spicy flavour of ginger mint adds a hint of the orient to this succulent marinated chicken.

Serves 4

8 chicken thigh portions, skinned
15ml/1 tbsp clear honey
30ml/2 tbsp lime or lemon juice
30ml/2 tbsp natural yogurt
60ml/4 tbsp chopped fresh mint, preferably ginger mint
salt and ground black pepper
boiled potatoes and tomato salad, to serve

Slash the chicken flesh at intervals with a sharp knife. Place in a bowl. In another bowl mix together the honey, lemon or lime juice, yogurt, seasoning and half the mint.

Spoon the marinade over the chicken and leave to marinate for 30 minutes. Line the grill pan with foil and cook the chicken under a preheated moderately hot grill until thoroughly cooked and golden brown, turning occasionally.

Sprinkle the chicken with the remaining mint to garnish and serve with boiled potatoes and tomato salad.

CHICKEN WITH RED PESTO

Rich, robust flavours and strong colours topped with a basil garnish make this a memorable dish.

Serves 4

15g/½oz/2 tbsp plain flour
4 chicken legs, breasts or quarters
30ml/2 tbsp olive oil
1 onion, chopped
2 garlic cloves, chopped
1 red pepper, seeded and chopped
400g/14oz can chopped tomatoes
30ml/2 tbsp red pesto
4 sun-dried tomatoes in oil, chopped
150ml/¼ pint/⅔ cup chicken stock
5ml/1 tsp dried oregano
8 black olives, stoned
salt and ground black pepper
chopped fresh basil and basil leaves, to garnish
tagliatelle, to serve

Mix the flour with salt and pepper in a plastic bag. Add the chicken, close the bag tightly and shake until coated. Heat the oil in a flameproof casserole, add the chicken and brown quickly. Remove and set aside.

Lower the heat slightly and add the onion, garlic and red pepper. Cook for 5 minutes, then stir in the tomatoes, pesto, sun-dried tomatoes, stock and oregano. Bring to the boil.

Return the chicken to the casserole, season lightly, cover and simmer for 30–35 minutes, or until the chicken is cooked.

Add the olives and simmer for 5 minutes more. Transfer to a warmed serving dish, sprinkle with the chopped basil and garnish with basil leaves. Serve with hot tagliatelle.

CHICKEN WITH PARSLEY STUFFING

These little chicken drumsticks have a delectable herby flavour, in which parsley predominates.

Serves 4

60ml/4 tbsp ricotta cheese
1 garlic clove, crushed
30ml/2 tbsp chopped fresh parsley
15ml/1 tbsp mixed chopped fresh chives and tarragon
5ml/1 tsp mint
30ml/2 tbsp fresh brown breadcrumbs
8 chicken drumsticks
8 smoked streaky bacon rashers
5ml/1 tsp wholegrain mustard
15ml/1 tbsp sunflower oil
salt and freshly ground black pepper
chopped fresh parsley and chives, to garnish

Mix together the ricotta, garlic, herbs, breadcrumbs and seasoning. Carefully loosen the skin of each drumstick and spoon a little of the herb stuffing under the skin. Smooth the skin firmly over the stuffing.

Wrap a bacon rasher around the wide end of each drumstick, to hold the skin in place over the stuffing.

Mix together the mustard and oil and brush over the chicken. Cook over a medium-hot barbecue for about 25 minutes, turning occasionally, until the chicken is cooked through and the meat juices run clear. Serve garnished with chopped parsley and chives.

COOK'S TIP

If, thanks to the elements, you can't use the barbecue, cook indoors in the oven at 180°C/350°F/Gas 4 for 25–30 minutes, turning occasionally.

CHICKEN PARCELS WITH ROSEMARY

Rosemary butter is used to moisten tender chicken and to brush the filo pastry enclosing it.

Serves 4

4 chicken breast fillets, skinned
150g/5oz/⅝ cup butter, softened
90ml/6 tbsp chopped fresh rosemary
5ml/1 tsp lemon juice
5 large sheets filo pastry, thawed if frozen
1 egg, beaten
30ml/2 tbsp grated Parmesan cheese
salt and ground black pepper

Season the chicken fillets and fry in 25g/1oz/2 tbsp of the butter to seal and brown lightly. Allow to cool.

Preheat the oven to 190°C/375°F/Gas 5. Put the remaining butter, the rosemary, lemon juice and seasoning in a food processor and process until smooth. Melt half the herb butter.

Brush 1 sheet of filo pastry with herb butter. Fold it in half and brush again with butter. Place a chicken fillet about 2.5cm/1in from the top. Dot the chicken with a quarter of the remaining herb butter. Fold in the sides of the pastry, then roll up to enclose the filling completely. Place seam side down on a lightly greased baking sheet. Repeat with the other chicken fillets.

Brush the filo parcels with beaten egg. Cut the last sheet of filo into strips, scrunch and arrange on top. Brush the parcels with the egg glaze, then sprinkle with Parmesan. Bake in the oven for about 35–40 minutes.

COOK'S TIP

This recipe also works well with turkey breast fillets.

CHICKEN WITH SLOE GIN & JUNIPER

Juniper is used in the manufacture of gin and the reinforcement of the flavour, using both sloe gin and juniper, is delicious.

Serves 8

25g/1oz/2 tbsp butter
30ml/2 tbsp sunflower oil
8 chicken breasts, boned and skinned
4 carrots, sliced
1 garlic clove, crushed
15ml/1 tbsp finely chopped parsley
60ml/4 tbsp chicken stock
60ml/4 tbsp red wine
60ml/4 tbsp sloe gin
5ml/1 tsp crushed juniper berries
salt and ground black pepper
shredded fresh basil, to garnish

Melt the butter with the oil in a large frying pan. Fry the chicken breasts until they are brown on all sides then transfer to a shallow ovenproof dish or casserole.

Cook the carrots in a saucepan of lightly salted boiling water until tender. Drain and place in a food processor or in a blender. Add the garlic, parsley, stock, wine, gin and juniper berries. Process the carrot mixture to a smooth purée. Pour the sauce over the top of the chicken, then cover and simmer over a low heat for about 30 minutes or until the chicken is cooked through. Season to taste. Transfer to a serving dish and serve immediately, garnished with shredded fresh basil.

Chicken with Blackberries and Lemon

This delicious stew combines some wonderful flavours and the inclusion of red wine and blackberries gives it a dramatic appearance.

Serves 4

4 chicken breasts
25g/1oz/2 tbsp butter
15ml/1 tbsp sunflower oil
60ml/4 tbsp plain flour
150ml/¼ pint/⅔ cup red wine
150ml/¼ pint/⅔ cup chicken stock
grated rind and juice of ½ orange
3 lemon balm sprigs, finely chopped
150ml/¼ pint/⅔ cup double cream
1 egg yolk
115g/4oz/⅔ cup fresh blackberries
salt and ground black pepper
chopped lemon balm and fresh blackberries, to garnish

Preheat the oven to 180°C/350°F/Gas 4. Trim the chicken breasts, removing any skin. Heat the butter and oil in a large frying pan. Fry the chicken until sealed on all sides, then transfer to a casserole. Stir the flour into the remaining fat. Cook for 1 minute, stir in the wine and stock. Heat, stirring until the sauce thickens. Add the orange rind, juice, and the lemon balm. Pour over the chicken. Cover and cook in the oven for 40 minutes.

In a bowl, whisk the cream with the egg yolk and some of the liquid from the casserole; stir into the casserole. Add the blackberries. Cover and cook for 15 minutes. Garnish with lemon balm and blackberries.

Chicken, Leek and Parsley Pie

This is a classic English country dish. The creamy parsley sauce is the perfect complement to the chicken and leeks, bound together in an exquisite whole with wonderful melt-in-the-mouth pastry.

Serves 4–6

3 part-boned chicken breasts
flavouring ingredients (bouquet garni, black peppercorns, onion and carrot)
50g/2oz/4 tbsp butter
2 leeks, thinly sliced
50g/2oz/½ cup Cheddar cheese, grated
25g/1oz/⅓ cup Parmesan cheese, grated
45ml/3 tbsp chopped fresh parsley
30ml/2 tbsp wholegrain mustard
5ml/1 tsp cornflour
300ml/½ pint/1¼ cups double cream
salt and freshly ground black pepper
beaten egg, to glaze
mixed green salad, to serve

For the pastry

275g/10oz/2½ cups plain flour
200g/7oz/scant 1 cup butter, diced
2 egg yolks
pinch of salt

Make the pastry. Sift the flour and salt into a bowl. Blend the butter and egg yolks in a food processor until creamy. Add the flour and process very briefly until the mixture is just coming together. Add about 15ml/1 tbsp cold water and process for a few seconds more. Turn out on to a lightly floured surface and knead lightly. Wrap in clear film and chill for about 1 hour.

Meanwhile, place the chicken breasts in a single layer in a frying pan. Add the flavouring ingredients and enough water to just cover. Cover the pan with a lid and simmer very gently for about 20–25 minutes until the chicken is tender. Leave to cool in the liquid.

Preheat the oven to 200°C/400°F/Gas 6. Divide the pastry into two pieces, one slightly larger than the other. Roll out the larger piece on a lightly floured surface and use to line a 28 x 18cm/11 x 7in baking dish or tin. Prick the base with a fork and bake in the oven for 15 minutes. Leave to cool.

Discard the skin and bones from the chicken and cut the flesh into strips. Melt the butter in a frying pan and fry the leeks over a low heat until soft, stirring occasionally. Stir in the cheeses and parsley. Spead half the leek mixture over the cooked pastry base, cover with the chicken strips and then top with the remaining leek mixture. Mix together the mustard, cornflour and cream in a small bowl. Add seasoning to taste and pour over the filling.

Moisten the edges of the cooked pastry base. Roll out the remaining pastry and cover the pie. Brush with beaten egg and bake in the oven for 30–40 minutes until crisp and golden. Serve hot with a mixed green salad.

CHICKEN FRICASSEE FORESTIER

Chicken, wild mushrooms and lashings of parsley make this a truly splendid dish, perfect for a special meal, yet surprisingly easy and quick to make.

Serves 4

3 boned chicken breasts, sliced
15ml/1 tbsp sunflower oil
50g/2oz/4 tbsp butter
115g/4oz unsmoked streaky bacon, chopped
75ml/5 tbsp dry sherry or white wine
1 onion, chopped
350g/12oz assorted wild and cultivated mushrooms, sliced
40g/1½oz/3 tbsp plain flour
500ml/18fl oz/2¼ cups chicken stock
10ml/2 tsp lemon juice
60ml/4 tbsp chopped fresh parsley
salt and freshly ground black pepper
boiled rice, carrots and baby sweetcorn, to serve

COOK'S TIP

It is worth spending a little extra on free-range chicken for the low fat content and good flavour and texture of the meat.

Season the chicken with a little pepper. Heat the oil and half of the butter in a large frying pan or flameproof casserole and brown the chicken and bacon pieces. Transfer to a dish and pour off any excess fat. Return the pan to the heat and brown the sediment. Pour in the sherry or wine, stir with a wooden spoon to deglaze the pan and then pour the liquid over the chicken. Wipe the pan clean.

Fry the onion in the remaining butter until golden brown. Add the mushrooms and cook, stirring frequently, for 6–8 minutes. Reduce the heat, stir in the flour and then gradually add the chicken stock, stirring to make a smooth sauce.

Add the reserved chicken and bacon together with the sherry juices and heat until simmering. Simmer for 10–15 minutes until the chicken is cooked, then add the lemon juice, parsley (reserve a little parsley to scatter over the rice if you wish) and seasoning. Serve with plain boiled rice, carrots and baby sweetcorn.

Chicken Liver Stir-fry with Rosemary

The final sprinkling of lemon, rosemary and garlic gives this quick, easy and inexpensive dish a delightful fresh flavour and wonderful aroma.

Serves 4

500g/1¼ lb chicken livers
75g/3oz/6 tbsp butter
175g/6oz field mushrooms
50g/2oz chanterelle mushrooms
3 cloves of garlic, finely chopped
2 shallots, finely chopped
150ml/¼ pint/⅔ cup medium sherry
3 fresh rosemary sprigs
rind of 1 lemon, cut into thin strips
30ml/2 tbsp chopped fresh rosemary
salt and ground black pepper
flat leaf parsley, to garnish
4 thick slices white toast, to serve

Clean and trim the chicken livers to remove any gristle or muscle. Season them generously with salt and pepper, tossing well to coat thoroughly.

Heat a wok or heavy-based frying pan and add 15g/½oz/1 tbsp of the butter. When it has melted, add the livers in batches (melting more butter where necessary but reserving 25g/1oz/2 tbsp for the vegetables) and flash-fry until golden brown. Drain with a slotted spoon and transfer to a plate, then place in a low oven to keep warm.

Cut the field mushrooms into thick slices and cut the chanterelles in half, depending on their size.

Re-heat the wok or frying pan and add the remaining butter. When it has melted, stir in two-thirds of the chopped garlic and the shallots and stir-fry for 1 minute until golden brown. Stir in the mushrooms and continue to cook for a further 2 minutes.

Add the sherry, bring to the boil and simmer for 2–3 minutes until syrupy. Add 3 rosemary sprigs, salt and pepper and return the livers to the pan. Stir-fry for 1 minute. Sprinkle with a mixture of lemon rind, chopped rosemary and the remaining chopped garlic, garnish with flat leaf parsley and serve with slices of toast.

Stir-fried Chicken with Basil

The spicy, sharp flavour of Thai basil is the secret ingredient in this wonderful dish.

Serves 4–6

45ml/3 tbsp vegetable oil
4 garlic cloves, sliced
2–4 red chillies, seeded and chopped
450g/1lb chicken, cut into bite-size pieces
30–45ml/2–3 tbsp fish sauce
10ml/2 tsp dark soy sauce
5ml/1 tsp sugar
10–12 fresh Thai basil leaves

To garnish

2 red chillies, finely sliced
20 deep fried Thai basil leaves (see Cook's Tip)

Heat the oil in a wok or large frying pan, swirling it around carefully to coat the entire cooking surface. Add the garlic and red chillies and stir-fry until golden.

Add the chicken to the wok or pan; stir-fry until it changes colour.

Season with fish sauce, soy sauce and sugar. Continue to stir-fry for about 3–4 minutes, or until the chicken is cooked. Stir in the fresh Thai basil leaves. Garnish with sliced chillies and deep fried basil.

Cook's Tip

To deep fry Thai basil leaves, make sure they are completely dry. Deep fry in hot oil for about 30–40 seconds, lift out and drain on kitchen paper.

TURKEY WITH BASIL AND PEPPER SAUCE

Turkey rolled up with a garlic and basil cream and served with a pepper sauce is a popular supper treat.

Serves 4

4 turkey escalopes

75g/3oz Boursin or garlic-flavoured cream cheese

12 fresh basil leaves

25g/1oz/2 tbsp butter

15ml/1 tbsp olive oil

salt and ground black pepper

For the yellow pepper sauce

15ml/1 tbsp olive oil

2 large yellow peppers, seeded and chopped

1 small onion, chopped

15ml/1 tbsp fresh orange juice

300ml/½ pint/1¼ cups chicken stock

COOK'S TIP

Skinless, boneless chicken breasts or veal escalopes could be used instead of the turkey.

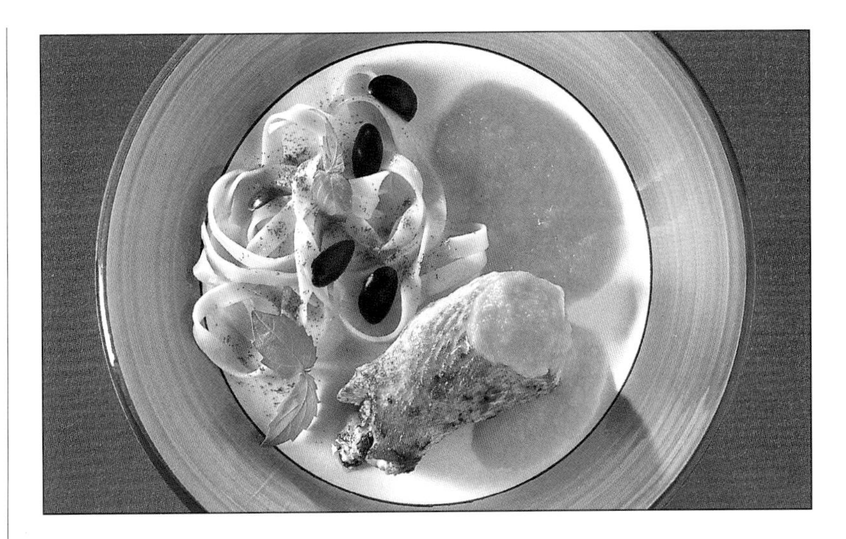

Make the yellow pepper sauce. Heat the oil in a saucepan and gently fry the peppers and onion until beginning to soften. Add the orange juice and stock and cook until the vegetables are very soft.

Meanwhile, lay the turkey escalopes on a board and beat them out lightly. Spread the escalopes with the cream cheese. Shred half the basil leaves and sprinkle on top, then roll up each escalope, tucking in the ends like an envelope, and secure neatly with half a cocktail stick.

Melt the butter with the oil in a frying pan. Fry the turkey rolls for about 7–8 minutes, turning them frequently, until golden and cooked.

Meanwhile, press the pepper mixture through a sieve until smooth, then return to a clean pan. Season the sauce to taste and warm through, or serve cold, with the escalopes, garnished with the remaining basil leaves.

Rosemary Duck and Chestnut Sauce

A sauce of sweet chestnuts complements duck breast that has been steeped in a herb and garlic marinade.

Serves 4–5

several fresh rosemary sprigs
1 garlic clove, thinly sliced
30ml/2 tbsp olive oil
4 duck breasts, boned and fat removed

For the chestnut sauce

450g/1lb chestnuts
5ml/1 tsp oil
350ml/12fl oz/1½ cups milk
1 small onion, finely chopped
1 carrot, finely chopped
1 small bay leaf
30ml/2 tbsp cream, warmed
salt and ground black pepper

Cook's Tip

The chestnut sauce may be prepared in advance and kept in the refrigerator for up to 2 days. It can also be frozen. Thaw before reheating.

Pull the leaves from 1 rosemary sprig. Combine them with the garlic and oil in a shallow bowl. Pat the duck breasts dry with kitchen paper and brush with the marinade. Allow to stand for at least 2 hours before cooking.

Meanwhile make the chestnut sauce. Preheat the oven to 180°C/350°F/Gas 4. Cut a cross in the flat side of each chestnut with a sharp knife. Place the chestnuts in a baking tin with the oil and shake the pan until the nuts are coated well. Bake in the oven for about 20 minutes. Allow to cool slightly, then peel.

Place the peeled chestnuts in a heavy-based saucepan with the milk, onion, carrot and bay leaf. Cook slowly for about 10–15 minutes until the chestnuts are very tender. Season with salt and pepper. Discard the bay leaf. Press the mixture through a sieve.

Return the sauce to the saucepan. Heat gently while the duck is cooking. Just before serving, stir in the cream. If the sauce is too thick, add a little more cream.

Preheat the grill or prepare a barbecue.

Grill the duck breasts until medium-rare, about 6–8 minutes. The meat should be pink when sliced. Slice into rounds and arrange on warmed plates. Serve with the heated sauce, garnished with the remaining rosemary sprigs.

meat dishes

Most beef, lamb and pork, whether of best quality or less expensive cuts, will gain flavour from the addition of herbs during cooking. Traditional partnerships, such as lamb and mint, are well catered for in this section, but why not try some of the more unexpected, but equally delicious combinations, like Rosemary and Juniper Beef Stew or Pork and Thyme Filo Parcels.

BEEF WELLINGTON

The parsley pancakes make an unusual and tasty addition to this popular dish. The traditional goose liver pâté is replaced here with a rich mushroom pâté.

Serves 4

675g/1½lb fillet steak, tied
15ml/1 tbsp sunflower oil
350g/12oz puff pastry, thawed if frozen
1 egg, beaten, to glaze
salt and freshly ground black pepper
watercress, to garnish

For the parsley pancakes

50g/2oz/4 tbsp plain flour
1 egg
150ml/¼ pint/⅔ cup milk
30ml/2 tbsp chopped fresh parsley

For the mushroom pâté

50g/2oz/1 cup fresh white breadcrumbs
75ml/5 tbsp double cream
2 egg yolks
25g/1oz/2 tbsp butter
2 shallots or 1 small onion, chopped
450g/1lb assorted wild and cultivated mushrooms, chopped

Preheat the oven to 220°C/425°F/Gas 7 and season the meat with black pepper. Heat the oil in a roasting tin, add the meat and brown on all sides. Transfer to the oven and roast for 15 minutes for rare, 20 minutes for medium-rare and 25 minutes for well-done meat. Set aside to cool. Reduce the oven temperature to 190°C/375°F/Gas 5.

Make the pancakes. Beat together the flour, a pinch of salt, the egg, milk and parsley to make a smooth batter. Heat a large non-stick frying pan and pour in enough batter to coat the bottom. When set, flip over and cook briefly until lightly browned. Continue with the remaining batter to make four pancakes.

Make the mushroom pâté. Blend together the breadcrumbs, cream and egg yolks. Melt the butter in a frying pan and fry the shallots or onion until slightly softened. Add the mushrooms and cook briskly until the juices begin to run and then evaporate. When the mushrooms are quite dry, stir in the breadcrumb mixture, blending to make a smooth paste. Allow to cool.

Roll out the pastry and cut into a rectangle 35 x 30cm/14 x 12in. Place two pancakes on the pastry and spread with mushroom pâté. Place the beef on top and spread over any remaining pâté. Cover with the remaining pancakes. Cut out four small squares from the corners of the pastry and reserve. Moisten the pastry edges and wrap over the meat.

Decorate the top with the reserved pastry trimming and transfer to a baking sheet. Brush the pastry evenly with beaten egg and cook for about 40 minutes until golden brown. Serve garnished with watercress.

STEAK & KIDNEY PIE WITH BAY GRAVY

This is a sharpened-up, bay-flavoured version of a traditional favourite. The fragrant mustard, bay and parsley gravy perfectly complements the flavour of the beef.

Serves 4

450g/1lb puff pastry
35ml/2½ tbsp flour
675g/1½lb rump steak, cubed
175g/6oz pig's or lamb's kidney
25g/1oz/2 tbsp butter
1 medium onion, chopped
15ml/1 tbsp made English mustard
2 bay leaves
15ml/1 tbsp chopped parsley
150ml/¼pint ⅔ cup beef stock
1 egg, beaten
salt and pepper

Roll out two-thirds of the pastry on a floured surface to about 3mm/⅛in thick. Line a 1.5 litre/2½ pint/6¼ cup pie dish. Place a pie funnel in the middle.

Put the flour, salt and pepper in a bowl and toss the cubes of steak in the mixture. Remove all fat and skin from the kidneys, core them and slice thickly. Add to the steak cubes and toss well. Melt the butter in a pan and fry the onion until soft, then add the mustard, bay leaves, parsley and stock and stir well.

Preheat the oven to 190°C/375°F/Gas 5. Place the steak and kidney in the pie dish and add the stock mixture. Roll out the remaining pastry to a thickness of 3mm/⅛in. Brush the edges of the pastry forming the lower half of the pie with beaten egg and cover with the second piece of pastry. Press the pieces of pastry together to seal the edges, then trim. With the trimmings decorate the top in a leaf pattern.

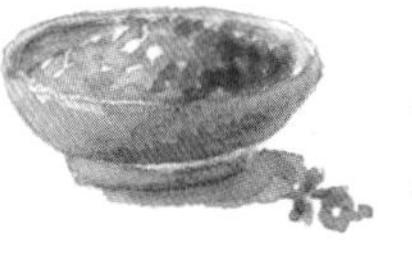

Brush the whole pie with beaten egg and make a small hole over the top of the funnel. Bake for about 1 hour until the pastry is golden brown.

ROSEMARY AND JUNIPER BEEF STEW

Marinating develops a rich base for casseroles and stews. Here, the complementary flavours of rosemary and juniper berries are dominant.

Serves 4–6

675g/1½lb chuck steak, trimmed and cut into 2.5cm/1in cubes
2 carrots, cut into batons
225g/8oz baby onions or shallots
115g/4oz button mushrooms
4 fresh rosemary sprigs
8 juniper berries, lightly crushed
8 black peppercorns, lightly crushed
300ml/½ pint/1¼ cups red wine
30ml/2 tbsp vegetable oil
150ml/¼ pint/⅔ cup stock
30ml/2 tbsp beurre manié
salt
broccoli, to serve

Place the meat in a bowl and add the carrots, onions or shallots, mushrooms, rosemary, juniper berries and peppercorns. Pour over the wine, cover and leave in a cool place for 4–5 hours, stirring occasionally.

Remove the meat and vegetables from the bowl with a slotted spoon and set aside. Strain the marinade into a jug.

Preheat the oven to 160°C/325°F/Gas 3. Heat the oil in a frying pan and fry the meat and vegetables in batches until lightly browned. Pour over the reserved marinade and stock and bring to the boil, stirring from time to time. Transfer to a casserole, cover and cook in the oven for 2 hours.

Twenty minutes before the end of cooking stir in the beurre manié, cover again and return to the oven. Season to taste and serve with broccoli.

COOK'S TIP

To make beurre manié, combine equal quantities of flour and butter.

BEEF AND CORIANDER RAGOUT

Based on the ever-popular couscous recipes of North Africa, this coriander-spiced ragoût mixes minced beef with a mixture of fresh vegetables.

Serves 4

15ml/1 tbsp oil
450g/1lb/4 cups minced beef
1 garlic clove, crushed
1 onion, quartered
30ml/2 tbsp plain flour
150ml/¼ pint/⅔ cup dry white wine
150ml/¼ pint/⅔ cup beef stock
2 baby turnips, chopped
115g/4oz swede, chopped
2 carrots, cut into chunks
2 courgettes, cut into chunks
15ml/1 tbsp chopped fresh coriander
5ml/1 tsp ground coriander
225g/8oz/1½ cups couscous
salt and ground black pepper
fresh coriander, to garnish

Heat the oil in a large saucepan. Add the minced beef and fry for 5 minutes, stirring frequently. Add the garlic and onion. Cook for a further 3 minutes, then stir in the flour. Cook for 1 minute. Add the wine and stock and bring to the boil, stirring all the time.

Add the prepared vegetables with the fresh and ground coriander. Stir in salt and pepper to taste. Lower the heat, cover and cook for 15 minutes.

Meanwhile, place the couscous in a bowl. Pour in boiling water to cover. Leave to stand for 10 minutes. Drain and place the couscous in a lined steamer or colander. Remove the lid from the saucepan containing the vegetables and place the steamer on top. Steam the couscous over the pan for 30 minutes more. Garnish with fresh coriander and serve.

Spicy Meatballs with Coriander

Coriander is the traditional flavouring for these tasty Indonesian meatballs.

Makes 24

1 large onion, roughly chopped
1–2 fresh red chillies, seeded and chopped
2 garlic cloves, crushed
1cm/½in cube terasi, prepared
15ml/1 tbsp coriander seeds
5ml/1 tsp cumin seeds
450g/1lb/4 cups lean minced beef
10ml/2 tsp dark soy sauce
5ml/1 tsp soft dark brown sugar
juice of ½ lemon
a little beaten egg
oil, for shallow frying
salt and ground black pepper
fresh coriander sprigs, to garnish

Cook's Tip

Terasi is a pungent shrimp paste, also known as blachan, kapi or ngapi. It should be heated gently before use.

Put the onion, chillies, garlic and terasi in a food processor or blender. Process in bursts; do not overmix or the onion will become too wet and spoil the consistency of the meatballs. Dry fry the coriander and cumin seeds in a preheated frying pan for about 1 minute, to release the aroma. Do not brown. Tip into a mortar and grind with a pestle.

Put the minced beef in a large mixing bowl. Stir in the onion mixture. Add the ground coriander and cumin, soy sauce, sugar and lemon juice. Stir in salt and pepper to taste, bind with a little beaten egg and shape into small, even-size balls.

Chill the meatballs briefly to firm them up, if necessary. Fry them in shallow oil, turning often, until cooked through and browned. This will take 4–5 minutes, depending on their size.

Remove from the pan with a slotted spoon, drain well on kitchen paper and serve, garnished with coriander sprigs.

SHISH KEBAB

This is one of the most famous dishes of the Arab world and it is cooked with lots of fresh parsley. Lamb is the traditional Moroccan meat for this dish, although beef can be used.

Serves 4

675g/1½lb lamb or beef
1 onion, grated
30ml/2 tbsp chopped fresh flat leaf parsley
5ml/1 tsp paprika
5ml/1 tsp ground cumin
15ml/1 tbsp olive oil
15ml/1 tbsp lemon juice
salt and freshly ground black pepper
fine strips of lemon rind and chopped fresh parsley, to garnish
Moroccan bread, lemon wedges, cumin seeds and cayenne pepper, to serve

Cut the meat into fairly small pieces, measuring approximately 2cm/¾in square. Mix the grated onion, parsley, paprika, cumin, oil, lemon juice and seasoning in a large bowl and add the meat. Stir so that the meat is coated thoroughly, then set aside for about 2 hours.

Prepare a barbecue or preheat the grill. Thread the meat on to metal skewers, allowing about six to eight pieces of meat per skewer. Grill or barbecue the meat a few centimetres from the heat for 6–8 minutes or until the meat is cooked through, basting occasionally with the marinade. Arrange the kebabs on a serving plate and garnish with fine strips of lemon rind and chopped fresh parsley. Serve with Moroccan bread, lemon wedges and dishes of cumin seeds and cayenne pepper.

COOK'S TIP

Moroccan cooks often intersperse lamb or beef fat with the meat, which adds flavour and keeps the meat moist. Alternatively, if using lamb, choose a more fatty cut.

Roast Leg of Lamb with Rosemary

Served with haricot or flageolet beans and rich gravy, this French-style roast is a homage to rosemary.

Serves 8–10

2.5–3kg/6–7lb leg of lamb
3 or 4 garlic cloves
olive oil
fresh or dried rosemary leaves
450g/1lb dried haricot or flageolet beans, soaked overnight in cold water
1 bay leaf
30ml/2 tbsp red wine
150ml/¼ pint/⅔ cup lamb or beef stock
25g/1oz/2 tbsp butter
salt and ground black pepper
watercress, to garnish

Preheat the oven to 220°C/425°F/Gas 7. Wipe the leg of lamb with damp kitchen paper and dry the fat covering well. Cut 2 or 3 of the garlic cloves into 10–12 slivers; then, with the tip of a knife, cut 10–12 slits in the lamb and insert the garlic slivers into the slits. Rub with oil, season with salt and pepper and sprinkle with rosemary.

Set the lamb on a rack in a shallow roasting tin and put in the oven. After 15 minutes, reduce the heat to 180°C/350°F/Gas 4 and continue to roast for 1½–1¾ hours (about 18 minutes per 450g/1lb) or until a meat thermometer inserted into the thickest part of the meat registers 57–60°C/135–140°F for medium-rare to medium meat or 66°C/150°F for well-done.

Meanwhile, drain and rinse the beans and put in a saucepan with enough fresh water to cover generously. Add the remaining garlic and the bay leaf, then bring to the boil. Reduce the heat and simmer for 45 minutes–1 hour or until tender.

Transfer the roast to a board and allow to stand, loosely covered, for 10–15 minutes. Skim off the fat from the cooking juices, then add the wine and stock to the roasting tin. Boil over a medium heat, stirring and scraping the base of the tin, until slightly reduced. Strain into a warmed gravy boat.

Drain the beans, discard the bay leaf, then toss the beans with the butter until it melts. Season with salt and pepper. Transfer the lamb to a serving dish, garnish with watercress and serve with the beans and the sauce.

ROAST LEG OF LAMB WITH BASIL PESTO

For this American speciality, lamb is marinated and baked under a fragrant basil blanket.

Serves 6

115g/4oz/2 cups fresh basil leaves
4 garlic cloves, roughly chopped
45ml/3 tbsp pine nuts
150ml/¼ pint/⅔ cup olive oil
50g/2oz/⅔ cup freshly grated Parmesan cheese
5ml/1 tsp salt, or to taste
1 leg of lamb, about 2.5kg/5½lb
cooked vegetables, to serve

Start by making the pesto. Combine the basil, garlic and pine nuts in a food processor or blender and process until finely chopped. With the motor running, slowly add the oil in a steady stream through the feeder tube. Scrape the mixture into a bowl. Stir in the Parmesan and salt.

Place the lamb in a roasting tin. Make several slits in the meat with a sharp knife and spoon some pesto into each slit. Rub more pesto over the surface of the lamb. Continue patting on the pesto in a thick, even layer. Cover and allow to stand for 2 hours at room temperature, or overnight in the fridge.

Preheat the oven to 180°C/350°F/Gas 4. Transfer the roasting tin to the oven and roast the lamb, allowing about 20 minutes per 450g/1lb for rare meat and 25 minutes per 450g/1lb for medium-rare. Turn the lamb occasionally during roasting.

Remove the lamb from the oven, cover it loosely with tented foil, and allow to rest for about 15 minutes before carving and serving with a selection of vegetables.

COOK'S TIP

Buy Parmesan in the piece and grate it yourself. The flavour will be superior to the pre-grated packed product.

LAMB WITH ROSEMARY AND MUSTARD

A rosemary and mustard marinade brings a wonderful flavour to this grilled or barbecued lamb.

Serves 6–8

115g/4oz Dijon mustard

1–2 garlic cloves, finely chopped

30ml/2 tbsp olive oil

30ml/2 tbsp lemon juice

30ml/2 tbsp chopped fresh rosemary or 15ml/1 tbsp crumbled dried rosemary

2.25kg/5lb leg of lamb, boned and butterflied

salt and ground black pepper

Combine the mustard, garlic, oil, lemon juice, rosemary, salt and pepper in a shallow glass or ceramic dish. Mix well together.

Add the leg of lamb, secured with skewers, and rub the mustard mixture all over it. Cover the dish and leave the meat to marinate at room temperature for at least 3 hours.

Preheat the grill or light the barbecue. Place the lamb flat on the rack and spread with any mustard mixture left in the dish. If grilling, set the lamb 10–12.5cm/4–5in from the heat. Cook under the grill or over charcoal until the lamb is crusty and golden brown on the outside, 10–15 minutes on each side for rare meat, 20 minutes for medium or 25 minutes for well done.

Transfer the lamb to a carving board and leave to rest for at least 10 minutes before carving into neat, but quite thick slices for serving.

PARSLEY-CRUSTED LAMB

Parsley and oatmeal make a wonderful crunchy coating for this elegant and succulent dish.

Serves 6

2 best-end necks of lamb, about 1kg/2¼lb each
finely grated rind of 1 lemon
60ml/4 tbsp medium oatmeal
50g/2oz/1 cup fresh white breadcrumbs
60ml/4 tbsp chopped fresh flat leaf parsley
25g/1oz/2 tbsp butter, melted
30ml/2 tbsp clear honey
salt and freshly ground black pepper
fresh parsley sprigs, to garnish
roasted baby vegetables, to serve

COOK'S TIP

Ask the butcher to remove the chine bone for you, which will make carving easier. Racks of lamb sold in supermarkets are normally "chined" already.

Preheat the oven to 200°C/400°F/Gas 6. Trim the racks of lamb so that about 2.5cm/1in bone at the top is exposed. Trim the skin and some of the fat from the outer side of the rack and score with a sharp knife.

Mix together the lemon rind, oatmeal, breadcrumbs, chopped parsley and seasoning and stir in the melted butter. Brush the fatty side of each rack with honey and press the oatmeal mixture evenly over the surface.

Place the racks in a roasting tin with the oatmeal sides uppermost. Roast for 40–50 minutes, depending on whether you like rare or medium lamb. Cover loosely with foil if browning too much. To serve, slice each rack into three and arrange on warmed serving plates with roasted vegetables, garnished with parsley sprigs.

BARBECUED LAMB WITH ROSEMARY

A traditional mixture of parsley, sage, rosemary and thyme – the herbs of the popular folk song – adds a really summery flavour to this simple lamb dish.

Serves 4

1 leg of lamb, about 1.75kg/4½ lb
1 garlic clove, thinly sliced
handful of fresh rosemary
handful of fresh flat leaf parsley
handful of fresh sage
handful of fresh thyme
90ml/6 tbsp dry sherry
60ml/4 tbsp walnut oil
500g/1¼lb medium potatoes
salt and ground black pepper

Place the lamb on a board smooth side downwards, so that you can see where the bone lies. Using a sharp knife, make a long cut through the flesh down to the bone. Scrape away the meat from the bone on both sides, until the bone is completely exposed. Remove the bone and cut away any sinews and excess fat.

Cut through the thickest part of the meat to enable it to open out as flat as possible. Make several cuts in the lamb with a sharp knife, and push slivers of garlic and sprigs of herbs into them.

Place the meat in a bowl and pour over the sherry and oil. Chop about half the remaining herbs and scatter over the meat. Cover and leave to marinate in the refrigerator for at least 30 minutes.

Remove the lamb from the marinade and season. Place on a medium-hot barbecue and cook for 30–35 minutes, turning occasionally and basting with the reserved marinade.

Scrub the potatoes, then cut them in thick slices. Brush them with the marinade and place them around the lamb. Cook for about 15–20 minutes, turning occasionally, until they are golden brown.

COOK'S TIP

If you have a spit-roasting attachment for your barbecue (or oven), the lamb can be rolled with herbs inside, tied securely and spit roasted for 1½ hours. You can cook larger pieces of lamb on the spit.

MINTED LAMB SKEWERS

The perfect partnership of lamb and mint triumphs again in this recipe.

Serves 4

300ml/½ pint/1¼ cups Greek-style yogurt
½ garlic clove, crushed
good pinch of saffron powder
30ml/2 tbsp chopped fresh mint
30ml/2 tbsp clear honey
45ml/3 tbsp olive oil
3 lamb neck fillets, about 675g/1½lb
1 medium aubergine
2 small red onions, quartered
salt and ground black pepper
sprigs of fresh mint, to garnish
mixed salad and hot pitta bread, to serve

In a shallow dish, mix together the yogurt, garlic, saffron, mint, honey, oil and black pepper. Trim the lamb and cut into 2.5cm/1in cubes. Add to the marinade and stir until well coated. Cover and leave to marinate for at least 4 hours, or preferably overnight.

Cut the aubergine into 2.5cm/1in cubes and blanch in boiling salted water for 1–2 minutes. Drain well and pat dry on kitchen paper.

Remove the lamb cubes from the marinade. Thread the lamb, aubergine and onion pieces alternately on to skewers. Grill for 10–12 minutes under a preheated grill, turning and basting occasionally with the marinade, until the lamb is tender.

Serve the skewers garnished with mint sprigs and accompanied by a mixed salad and hot pitta bread.

COOK'S TIP

If you are using bamboo skewers, soak them in cold water before use to prevent them burning.

Minty Lamb Burgers

These rather special burgers, flavoured with mint and stuffed with melting mozzarella cheese, take a little extra time to prepare, but are well worth it. Redcurrant chutney makes an unusual accompaniment.

Serves 4

500g/1¼lb lean minced lamb
1 small onion, finely chopped
30ml/2 tbsp finely chopped fresh mint
30ml/2 tbsp finely chopped fresh parsley
115g/4oz mozzarella cheese
salt and ground black pepper
oil, for brushing

For the chutney

115g/4oz/1½ cups fresh or frozen redcurrants
10ml/2 tsp clear honey
5ml/1 tsp balsamic vinegar
30ml/2 tbsp finely chopped fresh mint

Mix together the lamb, onion, mint and parsley until evenly combined; season well with salt and pepper. Divide the mixture into eight equal pieces and use your hands to press them into flat rounds.

Cut the mozzarella into 4 slices or cubes. Place them on 4 of the lamb rounds. Top each with another round of meat mixture. Press together firmly, making 4 flattish burger shapes and sealing in the cheese completely.

Place all the ingredients for the chutney in a bowl and mash them together with a fork. Season well with salt and pepper.

Brush the lamb patties with oil and cook them over a moderately hot barbecue for about 15 minutes, turning once, until golden brown. Serve with the redcurrant chutney.

Lebanese Kibbeh with Minted Dip

Kibbeh is a kind of Middle Eastern meatloaf made from minced lamb and bulgur wheat, here served with a creamy minted yogurt dip.

Serves 6

115g/4oz/⅔ cup bulgur wheat
450g/1lb finely minced lean lamb
1 large onion, grated
15ml/1 tbsp melted butter
salt and ground black pepper
sprigs of fresh mint, to garnish
cooked rice, to serve

For the filling

30ml/2 tbsp oil
1 onion, finely chopped
225g/8oz minced lamb or veal
50g/2oz/½ cup pine nuts
2.5ml/½ tsp ground allspice

For the yogurt dip

600ml/1 pint/2½ cups Greek-style yogurt
2–3 garlic cloves, crushed
15–30ml/1–2 tbsp chopped fresh mint

Preheat the oven to 190°C/375°F/Gas 5. Rinse the bulgur wheat in a sieve and squeeze out the excess moisture.

Mix the lamb, onion and seasoning, kneading the mixture to make a thick paste. Add the bulgur wheat and blend together.

To make the filling, heat the oil in a frying pan and fry the onion until golden. Add the lamb or veal and cook, stirring, until evenly browned. Add the pine nuts, allspice and salt and pepper.

Oil a large baking dish and spread half of the meat and bulgur wheat mixture over the bottom. Spoon over the filling and top with a second layer of meat and bulgur wheat, pressing down firmly with the back of a spoon. Pour the melted butter over the top and bake in the oven for 40–45 minutes until browned on top.

Meanwhile make the yogurt dip: blend together the yogurt and garlic, spoon into a serving bowl and sprinkle with the chopped mint.

Cut the cooked kibbeh into squares or rectangles and serve garnished with mint sprigs and accompanied by cooked rice and the yogurt dip.

MARSALA PORK WITH ROSEMARY

Usually used in desserts, here Sicilian marsala partners aromatic rosemary to flavour pork escalopes.

Serves 4

25g/1oz dried cep or porcini mushrooms
4 pork escalopes
10ml/2 tsp balsamic vinegar
8 garlic cloves
15g/½oz/1 tbsp butter
45ml/3 tbsp marsala
several fresh rosemary sprigs
10 juniper berries, crushed
salt and ground black pepper
cooked noodles and green vegetables, to serve

Cook's Tip

Use good-quality pork escalopes that will not be submerged by the strong flavour of this unusual sauce.

Put the dried mushrooms in a bowl and just cover with hot water. Leave to stand.

Brush the pork with 5ml/1 tsp of the vinegar and season with salt and pepper. Put the garlic cloves in a small pan of boiling water and cook for 10 minutes until soft. Drain and set aside.

Melt the butter in a large frying pan. Add the pork and fry quickly until browned on the underside. Turn the meat over and cook for another minute.

Drain the mushrooms in a fine sieve and reserve the soaking liquid. Add the mushrooms and 60ml/4 tbsp of the reserved liquid to the pork, followed by the marsala, rosemary, garlic cloves, juniper berries and remaining vinegar. Simmer gently for about 3 minutes until the pork is cooked through. Season lightly and serve hot with noodles and green vegetables.

Honey-roast Pork with Rosemary

Rosemary, thyme and honey add flavour and sweetness to pork tenderloin, while mustard brings piquancy.

Serves 4

30ml/2 tbsp clear honey
30ml/2 tbsp Dijon mustard
5ml/1 tsp chopped fresh rosemary
2.5ml/½ tsp chopped fresh thyme
450g/1lb pork tenderloin, trimmed of any fat
1.5ml/¼ tsp pink and green peppercorns, crushed
fresh rosemary and thyme sprigs, to garnish
potato gratin and steamed cauliflower, to serve

For the red onion confit

4 red onions
350ml/12fl oz/1½ cups vegetable stock
15ml/1 tbsp red wine vinegar
15ml/1 tbsp caster sugar
1 garlic clove, crushed
30ml/2 tbsp ruby port
pinch of salt

Preheat the oven to 180°C/350°F/Gas 4.

Mix together the honey, mustard, rosemary and thyme in a small bowl. Spread the mixture over the pork and sprinkle with the peppercorns. Place in a non-stick roasting pan and cook in the oven for 35–45 minutes.

For the red onion confit, slice the onions into rings and put them into a heavy-based saucepan. Add the stock, vinegar, sugar and garlic clove, bring to the boil, then reduce the heat. Cover and simmer for 15 minutes.

Uncover the pan, pour in the port and continue to simmer, stirring occasionally, until the onions are soft and the juices thick and syrupy. Season to taste with salt.

Cut the pork into slices and arrange on 4 warmed plates. Serve, garnished with fresh rosemary and thyme sprigs, with the red onion confit, potato gratin and cauliflower.

ROAST PORK WITH SAGE & MARJORAM

Pork is an inexpensive choice which is equally suitable for a family dinner or a celebration meal. The fruity purée makes a delicious change from the more usual plain apple sauce.

Serves 8

2.75kg/6lb leg of pork
45ml/3 tbsp sage leaves
15ml/1 tbsp marjoram leaves
45ml/3 tbsp chopped celery leaves
60ml/4 tbsp cider
salt and ground black pepper

For the apple purée

15g/½oz/1 tbsp butter
2 eating apples
2 bananas
15ml/1 tbsp Calvados

COOK'S TIP

Herbs are widely used in meat dishes to add extra flavour. Although sage and marjoram are classic accompaniments to pork, thyme or rosemary would be equally good.

Preheat the oven to 180°C/350°F/Gas 4. Strip the rind from the pork, leaving an even layer of fat. Cut a piece of foil large enough to enclose the pork and place the leg in the centre. In a bowl, mix the sage, marjoram and celery leaves together. Cover the pork fat with the herb mixture, season to taste and wrap tightly. Place the foil package on a wire rack in a roasting tin. Roast for 2 hours. Fold back the foil and drizzle the cider over the pork, taking care not to disturb the herb coating. Continue cooking for 1–1½ hours, until a small sharp knife pressed into the thickest part of the joint produces clear juices.

Make the apple purée. Melt the butter in a small saucepan. Peel, quarter and core the apples and slice them into the pan. Turn to coat the slices in butter, then slice the bananas into the pan. Sauté the fruit for 2 minutes. Add the Calvados and set it alight. When the flames die down, remove the mixture from the heat and purée it in a food processor or blender. Spoon the purée into a small jug or bowl and serve with the roast pork.

PORK AND THYME FILO PARCELS

Filo pastry is easy to use and delicious – the light, crisp wrapping makes a simple recipe into a celebration.

Makes 8

15ml/1 tbsp sunflower oil, plus extra for frying
5ml/1 tsp freshly grated ginger
275g/10oz pork fillet, finely chopped
6 spring onions, chopped
115g/4oz/1 cup chopped mushrooms
75g/3oz/½ cup chopped bamboo shoots
12 water chestnuts, finely chopped
10ml/2 tsp cornflour
15ml/1 tbsp soy sauce
10ml/2 tsp anchovy essence
10ml/2 tsp fresh thyme, chopped
8 large sheets filo pastry
25g/1oz/2 tbsp butter, melted
salt and pepper
thyme, to garnish

Heat the oil and fry the ginger for a few seconds and then add the pork. Stir well and cook until the colour changes. Add the spring onions and mushrooms and cook until tender. Add the bamboo shoots and water chestnuts.

In a small bowl, mix the cornflour with the soy sauce and anchovy essence. Add to the pan and stir well. Add the chopped thyme, season with salt and pepper, and cook until thickened.

Take a sheet of filo pastry and fold in half to make a square. Place two tablespoonfuls of filling across one corner and fold the corner over, then fold in the sides. Brush the folded sides lightly with a little melted butter to help the pastry stick. Complete the roll, and place it join side down on a cloth, then fold the cloth over the top to cover it. Finish all the rolls, putting each one in the cloth as it is made.

Heat some oil for semi-deep frying, and fry two to three rolls at a time until evenly browned. Drain on absorbent paper and serve hot, garnished with thyme.

PORK WITH PARSLEY DUMPLINGS

The parsley dumplings really give this rich stew a country-style flavour. The pork is cooked with prunes and apricots – a delicious fruity combination that goes beautifully with this meat.

Serves 6

115g/4oz/½ cup pitted prunes, roughly chopped
115g/4oz/½ cup dried apricots, roughly chopped
300ml/½ pint/1¼ cups dry cider
30ml/2 tbsp plain flour
675g/1½lb lean boneless pork, cubed
about 30ml/2 tbsp sunflower oil
2 onions, roughly chopped
2 garlic cloves, crushed
6 celery sticks, roughly chopped
475ml/16fl oz/2 cups chicken stock
12 juniper berries, lightly crushed
30ml/2 tbsp chopped fresh thyme
425g/15oz can black-eyed beans, drained
salt and freshly ground black pepper

For the parsley dumplings

115g/4oz/1 cup self-raising flour
50g/2oz/generous ⅓ cup vegetable suet
45ml/3 tbsp chopped fresh parsley

Soak the prunes and apricots in the cider for 20 minutes. Preheat the oven to 180°C/350°F/Gas 4. Season the flour with salt and pepper and dust the pork cubes, reserving any left-over flour. Heat the oil in a large flameproof casserole and brown the meat in batches, adding a little more oil if necessary. Transfer to a plate with a slotted spoon.

Add the onions, garlic and celery to the casserole and cook for 5–6 minutes until the vegetables are slightly softened, stirring occasionally. Add the reserved flour and cook, stirring, for 1 minute. Blend in the stock, stirring until smooth, then add the dried fruit and cider, juniper berries, thyme and seasoning. Bring to the boil and add the pork. Cover and cook in the oven for 50 minutes.

Just before the end of cooking, prepare the dumplings. Sift the flour into a bowl and stir in the suet and parsley. Add about 90ml/6 tbsp water and stir to make a dough. Form into six dumplings.

Stir the beans into the casserole and adjust the seasoning. Arrange the dumplings on the stew, cover and cook in the oven for a further 20–25 minutes until the dumplings are puffy and the pork is tender.

sweets and preserves

Herbs are not just for savoury dishes; they can also add an extra something to desserts and preserves. Mint is probably the best-known herb used in this way as it makes a superb combination with many fruits, but what could be more refreshing than Borage, Mint and Lemon Balm Sorbet, and how about Passion Fruit and Angelica Syllabub or Red Pepper and Rosemary Jelly?

Minted Raspberry Bavarois

A sophisticated dessert given extra elegance by the addition of fresh mint.

Serves 6

450g/1lb/5½ cups fresh or frozen and thawed raspberries
30ml/2 tbsp icing sugar
30ml/2 tbsp lemon juice
15ml/1 tbsp finely chopped fresh mint
30ml/2 tbsp/2 sachets powdered gelatine
75ml/5 tbsp boiling water
300ml/½ pint/1¼ cups custard
250ml/8fl oz/1 cup Greek-style yogurt
sprigs of fresh mint, to decorate

Reserve a few raspberries for decoration. Place the remaining raspberries, icing sugar and lemon juice in a food processor and process them until smooth. Press the purée through a sieve to remove the raspberry pips. Add the mint. You should have about 600ml/1 pint/2½ cups of purée.

Sprinkle 5ml/1 tsp of the gelatine over 30ml/2 tbsp of the boiling water and stir until the gelatine has dissolved. Stir into 150ml/¼ pint/⅔ cup of the fruit purée.

Pour this jelly into a 1-litre/1¾-pint/4-cup mould and leave the mould to chill in the refrigerator until the jelly is just on the point of setting. Tip the mould to swirl the setting jelly around the sides and then leave to chill until the jelly has set completely.

Stir the remaining fruit purée into the custard and yogurt. Dissolve the rest of the gelatine in the remaining water and stir it quickly into the custard mixture.

Pour the raspberry custard into the mould and leave it to chill until it has set completely. To serve, dip the base of the mould quickly into hot water and then turn it out and decorate it with the reserved raspberries and the mint sprigs.

PASSION FRUIT AND ANGELICA SYLLABUB

Passion fruit have a unique fragrance and flavour which makes this syllabub quite irresistible.

Serves 6

6 passion fruit

15ml/1 tbsp chopped crystallized angelica, plus more to decorate

grated rind and juice of 2 limes

120ml/4fl oz/½ cup white wine

50g/2oz/⅓ cup icing sugar

300ml/½ pint/1¼ cups double cream

150ml/¼ pint/⅔ cup Greek natural yogurt

Scoop out the flesh, seeds and juice of the passion fruit and divide between six serving dishes. Place the crystallized angelica in a food processor with the lime rind and juice, and blend to a purée.

In a large bowl, mix the lime purée with the wine and icing sugar. Stir until the sugar is dissolved.

Whip the double cream until it begins to form soft peaks and then gradually beat in the wine mixture – the cream should thicken slightly. Whisk in the yogurt. Spoon the cream mixture over the passion fruit, and refrigerate until ready to serve. Decorate with more crystallized angelica before serving.

COOK'S TIP

For a change, try using kiwi fruit – or other fruit that is similarly full of seeds – instead of passion fruit.

MINTED LEMON MERINGUE BOMBE

This easy ice cream will cause a sensation at a dinner party – it is unusual but quite the most delicious combination of tastes that you can imagine.

Serves 6–8

2 large lemons
150g/5oz/⅔ cup granulated sugar
150ml/¼ pint/⅔ cup whipping cream
600ml/1 pint/2½ cups Greek natural yogurt
2 large meringues
3 small sprigs fresh mint
225g/8oz good-quality mint chocolate, grated

Slice the rind off the lemons with a potato peeler, then squeeze them for the juice. Place the lemon rind and sugar in a food processor and blend finely. Add the cream, yogurt and lemon juice and process thoroughly. Pour the mixture into a mixing bowl and add the meringues, roughly crushed. Reserve one of the mint sprigs and chop the rest finely. Add to the cream and lemon mixture. Pour into a 1.2 litre/2 pint/5 cup glass pudding basin and freeze for 4 hours.

When the ice cream has frozen, scoop out the middle and pour in the grated mint chocolate, reserving a little for the garnish. Replace the ice cream to cover the chocolate and refreeze. To turn out, dip the basin in very hot water for a few seconds to loosen the ice cream, then turn the basin upside-down over the serving plate. Decorate with grated chocolate and a sprig of mint.

COOK'S TIP

To make a change, instead of using the mint chocolate, try orange, lemon or other types of chocolate.

JAPANESE FRUIT SALAD WITH MINT

This dessert was served in a Japanese department store. Although it sounds a little unusual, it works very well – the coffee flavour is excellent with the fruit.

Serves 6

12 canned lychees and the juice from the can
1 small fresh pineapple
2 large ripe pears
2 fresh peaches
12 strawberries
6 small sprigs of mint plus 12 extra sprigs to decorate
15ml/1 tbsp instant coffee granules
30ml/2 tbsp boiling water
150ml/¼ pint/⅔ cup double cream

Peel the fruit as necessary and chop into equal-sized pieces. Place all the fruit in a large glass bowl and pour on the lychee juice. Put the mint, coffee granules and boiling water in a food processor. Blend until smooth. Add the cream and process again briefly. Serve the fruit salad drained and chilled, with two small sprigs of mint on each plate, and the coffee sauce separately.

MINT AND FRUIT FOOL

Applemint can easily run riot in the herb garden; this is an excellent way of using up an abundant crop.

Serves 4–6

450g/1lb tart apples, peeled, cored and sliced
225g/8oz pink grapefruit segments
45ml/3 tbsp clear honey
30ml/2 tbsp water
6 large sprigs of fresh applemint, plus several small sprigs to garnish
150ml/¼ pint/⅔ cup double cream
300ml/½ pint/1¼ cups custard

Place the apples, grapefruit, honey, water and applemint in a pan, cover and simmer for 10 minutes until the apples are soft. Leave in the pan to cool, then discard the applemint. Purée the mixture in a food processor.

Whip the cream until it forms soft peaks, reserve 30ml/2 tbsp to decorate, if liked, and fold the rest into the custard. Carefully fold the custard into the apple and grapefruit mixture. Serve chilled in individual glasses, decorated with small sprigs of applemint.

Borage, Mint and Lemon Balm Sorbet

Borage has such a pretty flower head that it is worth growing just to make this recipe, and to float the flowers in summer drinks. The sorbet itself has a very refreshing, delicate taste, perfect for a hot afternoon.

Serves 6–8

500g/1¼lb/2⅛ cups sugar
500ml/17fl oz/2⅛ cups water
6 sprigs mint, plus extra to decorate
6 lemon balm leaves
250ml/8fl oz/1 cup white wine
30ml/2 tbsp lemon juice
mint sprigs, to decorate

Place the sugar and water in a saucepan with the washed herbs. Bring to the boil. Remove from the heat and add the wine. Cover and cool. Chill for several hours, then add the lemon juice. Freeze in a suitable container. As soon as the mixture begins to freeze, stir it briskly and replace in the freezer. Repeat every 15 minutes for at least 3 hours or until ready to serve.

To make the small ice bowls, pour about 1cm/½in cold, boiled water into small freezer-proof bowls, about 600ml/1 pint/2½ cups in capacity, and arrange some herbs in the water. Place in the freezer. Once this has frozen add a little more water to cover the herbs and freeze. Place a smaller freezer-proof bowl inside the larger bowl and put a heavy weight inside, such as a metal weight from some scales. Fill with more cooled boiled water, float more herbs in this and freeze. To release the ice bowls, warm each bowl with very hot water for a few seconds, then tip out the ice bowl. Spoon the sorbet into the ice bowls, decorate with sprigs of mint and serve.

STRAWBERRY MINT SPONGE

This combination of fruit, mint and ice cream is a real winner.

Serves 6–8

6–10 fresh mint leaves, plus extra to decorate
175g/6 oz/¾ cup caster sugar
175g/6 oz/¾ cup butter, plus extra to grease tin
175g/6 oz/1½ cups self-raising flour
3 eggs
1.2 litres/2 pints/5 cups strawberry ice cream
600ml/1 pint/2½ cups double cream
30ml/2 tbsp mint liqueur
350g/12oz/2 cups fresh strawberries

Tear the mint into pieces and mix with the caster sugar. Leave overnight. Grease and line a deep springform cake tin. Preheat the oven to 190°C/375°/F/Gas 5. Remove the mint from the sugar. Mix the butter and sugar and add the flour, then the eggs. Pile the mixture into the tin.

Bake for 20–25 minutes, or until a skewer or pointed knife inserted into the middle comes away clean. Turn out on to a wire rack to cool. When cool, carefully split horizontally into two equal halves.

Clean the cake tin and line it with clear film. Put the bottom half of the cake back in the tin. Spread on the ice cream and level the top. Put on the top half of the cake and freeze for 3–4 hours.

Whip the cream with the mint liqueur. Remove the cake from the freezer and quickly spread a layer of whipped cream all over it, leaving a rough finish. Put the cake back into the freezer until about 10 minutes before serving. Decorate the cake with the strawberries and place fresh mint leaves on the plate around the cake.

RED PEPPER AND ROSEMARY JELLY

Whole sprigs of fresh rosemary are suspended in this wonderful amber-coloured jelly.

Makes 1.75kg/4lb

450g/1lb tomatoes, chopped
4 red peppers, seeded and chopped
2 red chillies, seeded and chopped
fresh rosemary sprigs
300ml/½ pint/1¼ cups water
300ml/½ pint/1¼ cups red wine vinegar
2.5ml/½ tsp salt
900g/2lb/4½ cups preserving sugar with added pectin
250ml/8fl oz/1 cup liquid pectin

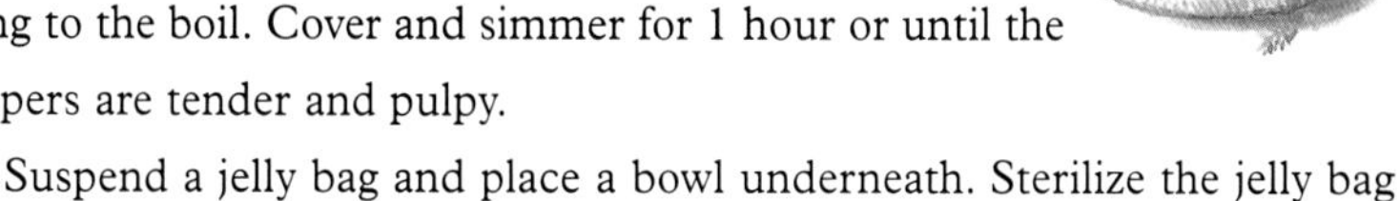

Place the tomatoes, peppers, chillies, a few rosemary sprigs and the water in a stainless-steel saucepan and bring to the boil. Cover and simmer for 1 hour or until the peppers are tender and pulpy.

Suspend a jelly bag and place a bowl underneath. Sterilize the jelly bag by pouring through boiling water. Discard the water and replace the bowl.

Pour the contents of the saucepan slowly into the jelly bag. Allow the juices to drip through slowly for several hours but do not squeeze the bag or the jelly will become cloudy. Sterilize the jars and lids required.

Place the juice in a clean saucepan with the vinegar, salt and sugar. Discard the pulp in the jelly bag. Heat the juice gently, stirring occasionally, until the sugar has dissolved. Boil rapidly for 3 minutes.

Remove the saucepan from the heat and stir in the liquid pectin. Skim the surface with a piece of kitchen paper to remove any foam.

Pour the liquid into the sterilized jars and add a sprig of rosemary to each jar. Place a waxed disc on the surface of each and seal with a lid of cellophane paper and an elastic band. Allow to cool, then label and decorate with ribbons. Store in a cool place.

APPLE AND MINT JELLY

This jelly is delicious served with garden peas as well as the more traditional roasted meats such as lamb.

Makes 3 x 450g/1lb jars

900/2lb Bramley cooking apples

granulated sugar

45ml/3 tbsp chopped fresh mint

Chop the apples roughly and put them in a preserving pan. Add enough water to cover. Simmer until the fruit is soft. Pour through a jelly bag, allowing it to drip overnight. Do not squeeze the bag or the jelly will become cloudy.

Measure the amount of juice. To every 600ml/1 pint/2½ cups of juice, add 500g/1¼lb/2¾ cups granulated sugar. Place the juice and sugar in a large pan and heat gently. Dissolve the sugar and then bring to the boil. Test for setting, by pouring about 15ml/1 tbsp into a saucer and leaving to cool slightly. If a wrinkle forms on the surface when pushed with a fingertip, the jelly will set. When a set is reached, leave to cool. Stir in the mint and pot in sterilized jars. Seal each jar with a waxed disc and a tightly fitting cellophane top. Store in a cool, dark place. The jelly will keep unopened for up to a year. Once opened, keep in the fridge and consume within a week.

COOK'S TIP

Many varieties of mint can be used, but applemint will lend a particularly subtle flavour to the apple jelly.

LEMON AND MINT CURD

Home-made lemon curd is infinitely tastier than the commercial variety. The addition of mint gives this version an interesting extra tang.

Makes about 1.5kg/3lb

6 fresh mint leaves
900g/2lb/4 cups caster sugar
350g/12oz/1½ cups butter, cut into chunks
rind of 6 lemons, thinly pared, in large pieces, and their juice
8 eggs, beaten

COOK'S TIP

Try experimenting with different types of mint or substitute oranges for lemons. Lemon curd is best made using the freshest of ingredients, so buy fresh eggs and try to find unwaxed lemons.

Place the mint leaves and sugar in a food processor and blend until the mint leaves are very finely chopped and combined with the sugar.

Put the mint sugar, butter, lemon rind, lemon juice and eggs into a bowl and thoroughly mix together.

Set the bowl over a pan of simmering water. Make sure that it does not touch the surface of the water or the eggs will scramble. Cook, whisking gently, until all the butter has melted and the sugar has dissolved. Remove the lemon rind.

Continue to cook in this way, stirring frequently, for 35–40 minutes or until the mixture thickens. Pour into sterilized glass jars, filling them up to the rim. Seal with waxed paper circles and cellophane lids secured with rubber bands. Add a label and tie short lengths of string around the top of the jars to decorate. This lemon curd should be used within 3 months and open jars should be stored in the refrigerator.

INDEX

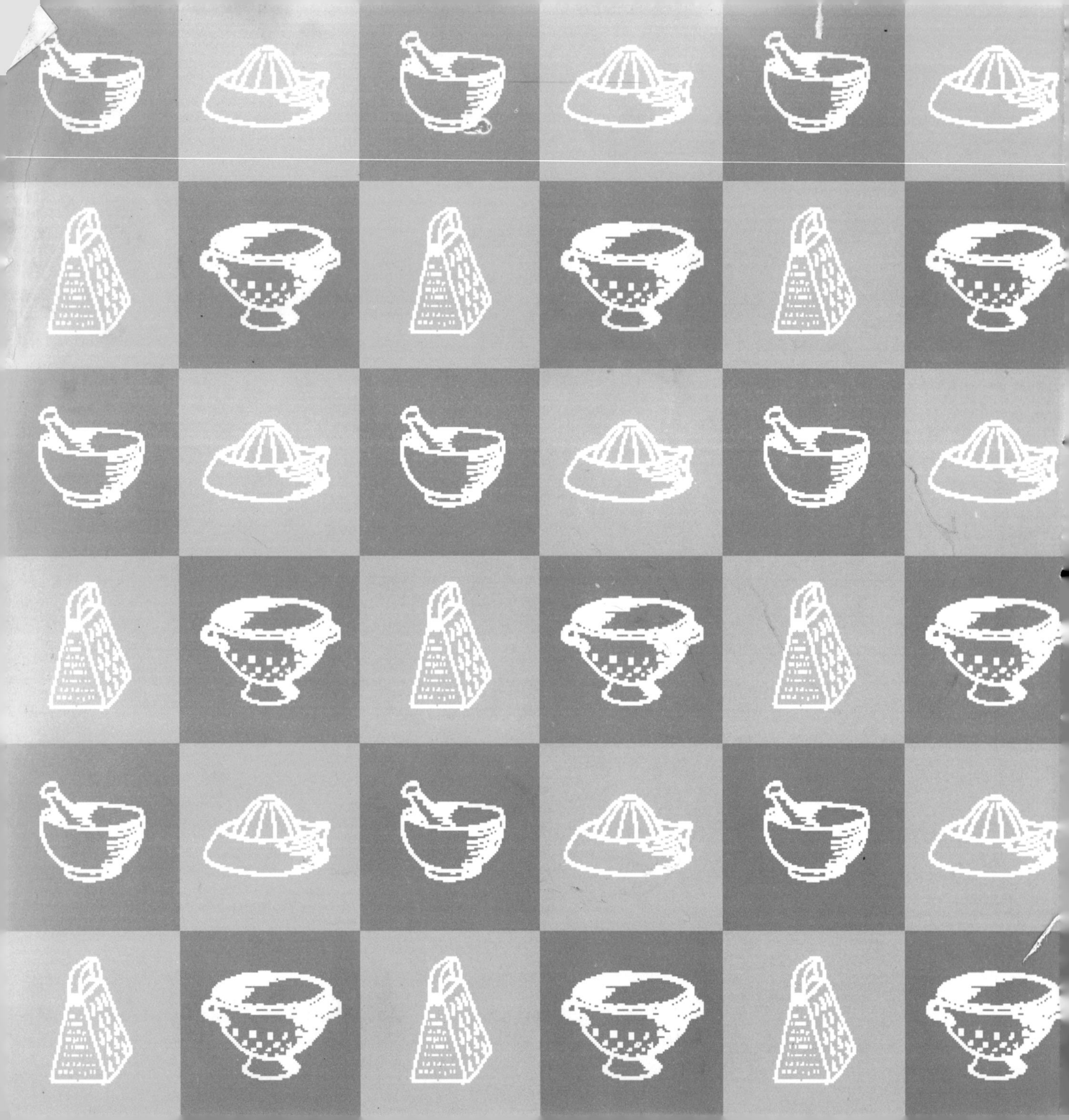